BRIGHT NOTES

LORD OF THE FLIES AND OTHER WORKS BY WILLIAM GOLDING

Intelligent Education

Nashville, Tennessee

BRIGHT NOTES: Lord of the Flies and Other Works
www.BrightNotes.com

No part of this publication may be used or reproduced in any manner whatsoever without written permission, except in the case of brief quotations in critical articles and reviews. For permissions, contact Influence Publishers http://www.influencepublishers.com.

ISBN: 978-1-645425-44-1 (Paperback)
ISBN: 978-1-645425-45-8 (eBook)

Published in accordance with the U.S. Copyright Office Orphan Works and Mass Digitization report of the register of copyrights, June 2015.

Originally published by Monarch Press.
Terence Dewsnap; Laurie Rozakis, 1964
2020 Edition published by Influence Publishers.

Interior design by Lapiz Digital Services. Cover Design by Thinkpen Designs.

Printed in the United States of America.

Library of Congress Cataloging-in-Publication Data forthcoming.
Names: Intelligent Education
Title: BRIGHT NOTES: Lord of the Flies and Other Works
Subject: STU004000 STUDY AIDS / Book Notes

CONTENTS

1)	Introduction To William Golding	1
2)	Lord of the Flies: Textual Analysis	6
	Chapter 1: The Sound Of The Shell	6
	Chapter 2: Fire On The Mountain	11
	Chapter 3: Huts On The Beach	15
	Chapter 4: Painted Faces And Long Hair	19
	Chapter 5: Beast From Water	23
	Chapter 6: Beast From Air	25
	Chapter 7: Shadows And Small Trees	28
	Chapter 8: Gift For The Darkness	31
	Chapter 9: A View To A Death	36
	Chapter 10: The Shell And The Glasses	39
	Chapter 11: Castle Rock	41
	Chapter 12: Cry Of The Hunters	44
3)	Lord of the Flies: Character Analyses	47
4)	Lord of the Flies: Essay Questions And Answers	56
5)	The Inheritors: Textual Analysis	65
	Chapter I	65
	Chapter II	67

	Chapter III	70
	Chapter IV	72
	Chapter V	74
	Chapter VI	76
	Chapter VII	78
	Chapter VIII	80
	Chapter IX	82
	Chapter X	84
	Chapter XI	86
	Chapter XII	88
6)	The Inheritors: Character Analyses	91
7)	Pincher Martin: Textual Analysis	95
	Chapters 1 and 2	95
	Chapters 3 and 4	97
	Chapters 5 and 6	99
	Chapters 7 and 8	101
	Chapters 9 and 10	103
	Chapters 11 and 12	105
	Chapters 13 and 14	107
8)	Pincher Martin: Character Analyses	109
9)	Free Fall: Textual Analysis	111
	Chapter I	111
	Chapter II	113
	Chapter III	115
	Chapter IV	117
	Chapter V	119
	Chapter VI	120
	Chapter VII	122
	Chapter VIII	124
	Chapter IX	126

	Chapter X	128
	Chapter XI	130
	Chapter XII	132
	Chapter XIII	134
	Chapter XIV	136
10)	Free Fall: Character Analyses	138
11)	Free Fall: Essay Questions And Answers	142
12)	Critical Commentary	153
13)	Bibliography	158

INTRODUCTION TO WILLIAM GOLDING

BACKGROUND

The literary career of William Golding (born in Cornwall in 1911) can be traced to two changes in his outlook. The first came after two years at Oxford University, when he abandoned his scientific studies for English literature, especially Old English poetry. He was graduated from Oxford with a B.A. in 1935. The second took form during World War II and concerns his view of human nature: Joining the British Navy in 1940, he participated in many important battles, including the Normandy invasion on D day, and by the end of the war, he was a lieutenant in command of a rocket warship. "When I was young, before the war, I did have some airy-fairy views about man," he said in "A Conversation with Golding" (Douglas M. Davis, *The New Republic*, May 4, 1963). "But I went through the war and that changed me. The war taught me different and a lot of others like me."

After the war he became a school teacher in Salisbury, England. For fifteen years "I read nothing but classical Greek, not because it was the snobbish thing to do or even the most enjoyable, but because this is where the meat is." During this period he wrote poetry, short stories, and a historical play, *The Brass Butterfly* (1958), as well as the novels that have made him famous: *Lord of the Flies* (1954), *The Inheritors* (1955), *Pincher Martin* (1956), and *Free Fall* (1959).

Golding owes the distinctive quality of his fiction to the influence of the Greek drama and **epic**. His use of the disheveled choirboys in *Lord of the Flies* and the inner voices of Pincher Martin and Sammy Mountjoy as choruses; his use of myth; his evocation of fate as a force directing human lives in opposition, often, to laws of probability; his use of tragic **irony**, where the destiny of an individual is patently obvious to everyone but the individual; his description of ritual processions and sacrifices: all of these elements from Greek literature contribute to the symbolic overtones of his novels.

REALISM

His novels are, in some respects, close to actuality. There is a realism in his rendering of physical detail, for example, his description of *Pincher Martin's* view of the ocean breaking over a rock: "He heaved over in the sea and saw how each swell dipped for a moment, flung up a white hand of foam then disappeared as if the rock had swallowed it." And the accuracy with which he depicts the visual scene carries over into his presentation of the mechanics of human behavior, particularly the psychology of fear. There is a further **realism** in his dependence on his own experience for documentation. *Lord of the Flies*, an account of the struggle for survival of a group of boys on a tropical island, depends on his accurate observation and recording, as schoolboy and teacher, of the behavior of boys. *The Inheritors*, in which the last eight members of a tribe of Neanderthal men meet a tribe of Homo sapiens and are destroyed, is based not only on his archeological readings and his knowledge of Old English **epic**, but on his experience of the terrors and tensions of war. *Pincher Martin*, about a sailor shipwrecked alone on a rock in the Atlantic, depends upon scenes witnessed by Golding in his years in the navy. *Free Fall* might seem to be far removed from the author's experience, since it is a study of the mind of a prisoner of war of the Germans. But the central figure, Samuel Mountjoy, is an artist by profession, is the same age, and has had an intellectual and political history similar to the author's.

SYMBOLISM

Although, like many authors, he utilizes his personal history, Golding is unique in the way that he uses the actual to build a structure of meaning. The symbolism of his novels is often more important than the action. Though the literal story is in itself interesting, his characters, images, and settings go beyond the merely literal, to represent universal truths about human nature and society.

LORD OF THE FLIES

Golding's first novel is more than a boyhood adventure story. The conflicts on the island are the ever present antagonisms of human society. The problems are the problems of the world. The evil thriving in the individual boy is the evil that threatens mankind. Two movements in the novel represent the two forces that govern society. The first is the tendency to orderliness represented in the parliamentary rules of the boys' meetings and in their attempts to build a signal fire. The second is the movement towards chaos as the fire gets out of hand or is forgotten, and as the boys participate in orgies of hunting, primitive dance, and even human sacrifice. The second force is the stronger; without the traditional protection of society, and without superior intellectual guidance the boys swing towards anarchy.

THE INHERITORS

The Inheritors is at first glance a mere primitive tale, though clearly based on serious linguistic, psychological, and anthropological research. But it gradually becomes apparent that the primitive story is a mirror for the contemporary age. The problems of the primitive society are contemporary. The struggle for survival by the last of the Neanderthals, as they encounter the more sophisticated tribe with their canoes and sharper weapons, is the situation of modern man confronted by technological advances in weapons and destructive chemicals. Just as Homo sapiens treated the Neanderthal with cruelty, so technology, according to Golding, produces a new potentiality for human cruelty in the modern world. His examination of the roots of personal and racial hatred leads him to suggest that the problem of man's inhumanity to man is not a new one, and that the need for reform is more than governmental; it must take into account the individual's natural proneness to evil.

PINCHER MARTIN

This is a survival novel dealing with the adventures of a shipwrecked sailor. But the question is not merely one of physical survival, but, more importantly, who is this man Christopher Martin? And what is he worth? Partially, the question is to be answered in terms of his personal characteristics-his toughness and greed. But more significant than these is his blind refusal to admit his guilt. He shuns the lobster that lurks by his island rock. He hates that kind of creature. But with his two claws reaching out to grab whatever soft morsel comes within his reach, he is a lobster. His tragedy is his lack of awareness. Like other Golding characters, he fails to use reason to control the violence in himself, because he does not know himself.

FREE FALL

Golding's fourth novel traces a quest for the meaning of life by a man representative of modern thought. After World War II, taking stock of his life, Samuel Mountjoy focuses on his experience as a war prisoner of the Germans. He knew at the time that he could be persuaded to give up information about his fellow prisoners, and that his nobility or infamy would be a result of circumstance and not choice. A representation of man in the prison of society and self who behaves according to machine-like impulses, he goes back over the history of his life in an attempt to solve the problem of why he acts the way he does. As he pursues the origins of his flawed character, he comes to the realization that the first cause of his fall was not in his poor environment but rather in himself. The first fall was free. And once he wastes the freedom possessed in childhood, his life becomes like the free fall of an object in space. Now that he possesses this knowledge, he recovers a sense of totality that enables him to give direction to his life.

GENERAL VIEW

Golding's novels raise the question of how violence and disorder are to be controlled in the modern world. If the novels do not contain an explicit solution to the problem, the implied answer is that man, who contains within himself the seeds of evil, also possesses the faculty of reason to control anarchistic impulses. The meaning of his symbolism is ultimately optimistic.

LORD OF THE FLIES

TEXTUAL ANALYSIS

CHAPTER 1: THE SOUND OF THE SHELL

A group of boys evacuated from England during an atomic war have landed on a tropical island in a "passenger tube" ejected from a flaming airplane. At first we see only two boys, Ralph, who is tall and fair-haired, and Piggy, his fat companion. But, when Ralph discovers a conch shell and blows it, a number of others struggle out of the jungle and gather on the beach. An election for chief is held, and Ralph wins over Jack, the leader of a group of black-robed choirboys. Ralph invites Jack and Simon, one of the choirboys, to join him in scaling a mountain. The view from the mountain fills the three boys with joy; they are the sole masters of the isolated island.

Comment

A remote jungle setting is useful to the author who wants to avoid the complexities of civilized society and focus' instead on simple issues (for example, whether Tarzan's wholesomeness will protect him from the machinations of the evil witch doctor). Similarly, the advantage of using children as characters is that they are, supposedly, innocent and unsophisticated human beings who make no attempt to hide their true selves. It is ironic that while Golding does focus on such fundamental **themes** as the conflict of good and evil and the passage from innocence to experience, he discovers in this lonely island many of the complex problems that afflict society in the great cities of the world. The cruelty with which the boys taunt Piggy for his fatness, his glasses, and his lack of physical dexterity is like the attitude of sophisticated society to the outsider. Pride, pretense, and jealousy are other adult faults that lurk beneath the innocent appearances of the boys.

In addition to these flaws, the boys contain elements of the nobility and heroism that have made positive contributions to the progress of western civilization. Simon represents a mystical, Piggy an intellectual, and Ralph a political hope for the lost boys. These leaders, along with the wielder of physical power, Jack, are faced with the same problems of survival as those of Defoe's Robinson Crusoe on his island. They must organize their lives to meet the threat to survival. Their problems contribute to suspense. Will they be able to make contact with other human beings? Will they be able to keep their group intact? And, more immediately, will they be able to find food and shelter?

The island, with a scar cut across it by the passenger tube, is a replica of the cities scarred by atomic warfare. That the atmosphere of violence should extend to this remote region is an indication of Golding's belief in the universality of evil.

The conch shell becomes a symbol of authority. The large, spiral shaped sea shell, its geometrical form created over a period of scores of years, is a fitting substitute on the island for the slowly evolved laws of human society. In Greek mythology Triton, the son of Neptune, uses the conch shell to stir or calm the seas. Here, Ralph, following the instructions of Piggy, uses the shell to subdue and control the animal spirits of the boys.

The mountain signifies many things for many people but generally represents the dignity of man as he aspires to spiritual freedom. To achieve the top of the mountain is to destroy fear and superstition and to gain mastery over nature.

Rock is a symbol of brute force. When Jack discovers a loose boulder while ascending the mountain, Ralph and Simon help him pry it loose. When the rock plummets down, "the forest further down shook as with the passage of an enraged monster. Wacco" shouts one boy. "Like a bomb!" cries another. With this **episode**, the realm of childish innocence of games and slang is broken by the intrusion of a destructive force. It is Jack who distracts the boys from their purpose of climbing the mountain and, for no reason except to create a make-believe "monster" or "bomb," causes them to release this violence. Jack's identity is here established. He is a leader who, like reckless leaders in the civilized world, prefers destruction to creation.

Notes

passenger tube - a removable compartment in the airliner of the future.

wacco - splendid.

wizard - excellent.

Character Analyses

Ralph - a representative type, the traditional fair-haired hero of boyhood adventure stories. His handsomeness and athletic ability make him a natural leader. For him the island seems to be the fulfillment of a schoolboy dream of adventure. Unfortunately his dream of adventure and hope of romantic rescue do not fit the reality of the difficult situation of the lost boys.

Piggy - an intelligent but physically deficient fat boy. He is one kind of modern man, a reader and thinker-not a doer. He longs for the authority and tradition of the grown-ups and the protection of the civilized world. He is out of place on the island because his asthma and constantly steamed glasses prevent him from carrying out plans to gather fruit or to find the other boys. He is a ready victim for any beast of prey and, as an outsider, an easy target for the scorn of the other boys.

Jack - a cruel and unpleasant looking bully. When he leads his choir out of the jungle, he forces them to remain in marching columns until one boy, Simon, faints. He constantly competes with Ralph for control of the boys. The only boy who carries a knife, at the end of the chapter he attempts to kill a piglet.

Simon - a poetic, religiously sensitive boy, given to fainting spells. Why does Ralph choose Simon for the expedition to the mountain? Possibly he feels that in Simon he has an ally whom he can dominate. Later we learn that Ralph is attracted to Simon because of his bright eyes which seem to indicate a lively personality. Whatever Ralph's reason, it is clear that Golding sees in Simon a view of life different from that of the other two boys. When the boys are coming down the mountain, Simon responds to the beauty of some strange bushes by describing them, "Like candles. Candle bushes. Candle buds." His is a poetical and mystical response to the natural world.

Sam and Eric - identical twins who later become Samneric.

Maurice - the second largest choirboy, "broad and grinning all the time."

Roger - a secretive, "slight, furtive boy."

LORD OF THE FLIES

TEXTUAL ANALYSIS

CHAPTER 2: FIRE ON THE MOUNTAIN

....

Ralph, conducting an organizational meeting on a granite platform above the beach, rules that anyone who wants to speak must first raise his hand, and then wait for the conch. While Ralph and Jack are attempting to reduce the worries of the boys by promising them a good time, a small boy shocks the assembly by announcing that a "snake-thing," a "beastie,"nfrightened him in the woods. Ralph channels the excitement of the boys into building a signal fire on the mountain. But, at the end of the chapter, the flames have crept into the forest, a fire is raging out of control, and the littl'un who saw the snake is missing.

Comment

The chapter begins in an attempt at order, with Ralph and Jack forming two branches of government. Ralph would make rules for the better conduct of the community's business. Jack, whose choirboys have now become "hunters," would happily enforce the rules by beating up anyone who disobeyed. With the establishment of a competitive relationship between the legislative and the military, the traditional conflict between civil and military authorities is prepared for.

Golding indicates the falseness of the optimism of the boys. When Ralph promises the boys a good time, "like in a book," the boys shout titles of adventure stories, including Coral Island, a novel by R. M. Ballantyne that, for generations, has been a favorite of English schoolboys. It tells of three boys on a desert island who survive through courage and cleverness. Ballantyne's characters, Ralph, the quiet, intelligent narrator, Jack, the dashing hero, and the merry Peterkin are models for Golding's leading characters, with both Piggy and Simon deriving from Peterkin. But, of course, Golding is ridiculing the easy solutions of the adventure story. Similarly, when Ralph promises that the boys will be rescued because the Queen has a room containing maps of all the islands of the world, he betrays his ignorance. He does not know that there are thousands of unmapped islands. He does not know that the Queen is a mere figurehead. His appeal to authority, to the grown-up world of Father, Navy, and Queen is in keeping with his storybook attitude to life. By the end of the chapter the false appearance of orderliness has been shattered. The movement from order to chaos is the pattern of the whole book and of most of the chapters.

The platform, raised above the danger and confusion of the jungle, and shaded comfortably, is an ideal location for parliamentary discourse. It represents a more rational level of human existence. In general, Golding uses **imagery** of height to represent some kind of human aspiration or mastery.

The snake, like the scar cut across the island by the "passenger tube" and like the rock dropped from the mountain, is an intrusion of the monstrous into the jungle paradise. Later we will learn that the snake is necessarily present wherever there are human beings because the snake-as a representation of evil-is part of man. This snake reminds us of another snake in another paradise. The author of Genesis, the first book of the Bible, describes the entrance of the Devil, in the form of a snake, into the Garden of Eden with the subsequent fall of Adam into sin. The snake that intrudes here is not the Devil, but represents a similar threat of evil. It injects fear and confusion into the precariously balanced world of the boys. It is a symbol, then, of the forces of disorder threatening society.

The fire often appears in opposition to the snake. The snake is a reminder of the limits of man. Sliding under rocks and through slime, it suggests the dark places of human experience. The fire is usually a symbol of the best in man. It represents the hopes of the human spirit as it flickers upward. For Ralph, who instigates confident of rescue because he believes that society still exists and that society takes an interest in him. In ancient Greek the making of the fire, it represents a faith in society. He is mythology, Prometheus, the son of a Titan, gave man fire. Ralph, in his eagerness to bring fire to the boys, is a modern Prometheus. When the fire rages out of control, it represents a different meaning. Piggy appropriately compares the fire at the end of the chapter to the fire of hell. What began as a cooperative effort has degenerated into a chaos of competitive bickering. Rational control was insufficient to withstand the impulses of the moment. If the leaders had been able to make use of Piggy's wisdom, they might have achieved some stability. But they are too reckless and unthinking. They are too interested in a momentary splurge of firelight, rather than the steady glow of reason, and the result is a destructive conflagration.

Piggy's glasses, which are snatched by the boys to light a fire, are representative of his intellectualism. He might be occasionally useful to the boys, but he will never have their respect. The author, by the way, has made a mistake in having the boys use Piggy's glasses to start a fire. The prescription for Piggy's myopia would be a concave lens, which scatters rather than concentrates the rays of light on a single point.

To reinforce the idea of evil lurking amid innocence, Golding uses a "running image," that is, a picture repeated several times in different places in the novel and usually acquiring symbolic significance. Here, the creeper, or jungle vine, is a "running image." On the first page of the novel Piggy is almost unable to move because he is tangled in creepers. Going up the mountain, the boys have difficulty getting through the creepers. When the small boys tells of the snake, one of the others suggests that it was only the creepers. In the fire that burns at the end of Chapter 2, a tree explodes and creepers shoot into the air. The little boys scream: "Snakes! Snakes! Look at the snakes!" The creepers suggest the same power of disorder present in the snake and released in the ravaging fire. They represent whatever impedes the progress of reason.

Notes

coign - a corner.

doink - probably the sound of striking a skull.

Character Analyses

The Little 'Uns - the mass of small boys, about six years old, who later are called Littluns. The "little 'un" who saw the "snake-thing" is distinguished by a large purple birthmark on the side of his face. Only a few of the "little 'uns" acquire distinct personalities.

LORD OF THE FLIES

TEXTUAL ANALYSIS

CHAPTER 3: HUTS ON THE BEACH

Several weeks have passed. Jack, almost naked, is crawling through the underbrush armed with a sharp stick. After a pig eludes him, he returns to the beach where Ralph and Simon are erecting precarious huts of palm leaves. When Simon disappears, Ralph and Jack agree that there is something "queer" about him. We see Simon pause to distribute fruit to the littluns, then slip into the depths of the jungle where, as evening approaches, he listens to the cries of jungle birds and gulls and to the sound of the surf.

Comment

The different purposes of the boys draw them apart, weakening the unity of the island society. Jack indulges his hunting instinct. Ralph accepts the responsibility of building housing for the boys. Simon finds fulfillment in a natural cell in the jungle. The society is also threatened by a demoralizing fear. The littluns scream in the night in terror of the snake-thing. And Jack admits that, at times when he is hunting, he senses something behind him in the jungle hunting him. Both fears are manifestations of a power within the boys that can destroy them. The dark terrors of the jungle reflect the dark parts of the human mind.

Notice especially, in this chapter, Golding's use of point of view-the outlook that an author assumes in narrating a story.

An author may select a character who refers to himself as "I" to tell the story. If so, the author must confine himself to things seen, heard, felt, and thought by that "I". Depending on whether the narrator is the main character or some minor character, this point of view is called "first person **protagonist**" or "first person witness." A story may be told by an author who looks at everything from the point of view of one character who is referred to as he or is identified by a proper name. This is the "third person" or "limited omniscient author" point of view. Or an author may allow himself to go into anyone's mind and to make what editorial comments he likes. This is the "omniscient author" point of view. This is Golding's point of view. Although he differs from some omniscient authors, for example Dickens, in that he seldom makes comments of his own, but rather chooses to see events through the eyes of his characters, he allows himself the omniscient author's freedom to move from person to person. Thus, in this chapter he is able to explore the thicket with Jack, report the conversation on the beach between Ralph, Simon, and Jack, and, finally, follow Simon on his solitary pilgrimage. Read the chapter closely, noticing how he observes the actions of Jack and the dialogue of the boys mostly from the outside, and then goes inside the mind of Simon in the jungle, seeing, hearing, and feeling the same things that he does. We tend to respond more sympathetically to a character whose mind we enter.

The huts that Ralph is constructing are necessary to survival. But although in adventure stories the hero is able to whip together sturdy shelters of palm leaves, such huts are actually difficult architectural projects requiring more than the haphazard efforts of adventuresome boys. The collapsing of the hut represents the failure of civilization on the island.

Notes

crackers - crazy.

node - the raised joint where the tendril attaches to the vine.

sepals - the green leaves that constitute the external part of a flower.

susurration - whispering sound.

tendril - the string-like projections of a vine that grip supporting objects.

trotters - feet.

Character Analyses

Ralph - Although he criticizes the others for their lack of cooperation, Ralph himself must bear a large part of the responsibility for failure. Though he has the desire to bring civilization to the island, he lacks the competence of an effective organizer. His difficulties with the huts are a result of his simplifying and romanticizing the role of architect. His leadership weakens because he holds too idealized a view of life on the island.

Jack - has degenerated from a civilized English schoolboy to a primitive creature obsessed with the hunt. The methods of the chase come to him as naturally as to an animal as he sniffs the air for the scent of his prey. The urge to kill takes over his personality. Yet, he has not killed a single animal. He is finding a great difference between imagining oneself a hunter and actually killing a living creature. The act of violence demands a complete commitment.

Simon - His cheerfulness and loyalty are apparent when he helps Ralph and when he feeds the littluns. But his glittering black eyes hold more than youthful gaiety. His visit to the hut in the jungle where the beauty of nature is a symbol of the beauty of the spirit is like the journey of a religious man to a forest hermitage. He is a mystic as well as a poet, and he finds in the natural hut a security that he could not find in Ralph's huts on the beach. His admiration for the beautiful candle-like bushes and his sudden disappearance show him to be unlike the other boys and hence, from their point of view, "queer." In a practical society the love of beauty and solitude seem "queer." But later Simon is to derive from his meditations the strength to face the "beast" that menaces the island.

LORD OF THE FLIES

TEXTUAL ANALYSIS

CHAPTER 4: PAINTED FACES AND LONG HAIR

After he and Maurice have kicked over the sand castles of the littluns, Roger stalks one of the littluns and throws stones in his direction. Then the scene changes to another part of the jungle where Jack is painting his face with red and white clay and black charcoal. After Jack has led his hunters off into the jungle, Ralph sights smoke on the horizon. To his horror he discovers that the signal fire, which Jack's group had promised to tend, has gone out. When Jack and his hunters return triumphantly carrying a pig on a stake, Ralph and Piggy berate them until Jack turns on Piggy, knocking him down and breaking one of the lenses in his glasses. Finally, Ralph calls a meeting.

Comment

The smashing of the sand castles is a manifestation of the violence that can become the rule of the island. The older boys, instead of aiding the young, crush their castles, and with them their dreams of kings, queens, and noble knights. The older boys are not yet completely uncivilized though. Maurice feels guilty and runs away. Roger, when he pursues one of the littluns, is unable to throw rocks directly at him because the laws of school, church, and home restrain him. To throw rocks at a fellow human being is to return to an age when the law of survival was the only law governing brute man. Yet, under the layers of civilization, in the English schoolboy throbs the same instinct to kill that flourished in prehistoric times. And with the nourishing of this instinct, the civilization of the boys fails. The signal fire is allowed to die. A chance of rescue is lost. The energies of the boys are channeled into the one activity of hunting.

As the primitivism of the boys becomes more prevalent, as Jack turns on his fellow human being, Piggy, the cause of rationality seems doomed. The leadership of Ralph gives way to that of Jack. Ralph's success depends on his sensible response to the advice of Piggy and on his ability to make his image of the romantic hero attractive to the boys. If the boys become a tribe of frenzied savages, they will find the civilized manner of Ralph antagonistic. At the end of the chapter he calls a meeting to stave off Jack's threat to his leadership. But will the rules of parliamentary procedure be sufficient to check a revolution?

The pig dance is a symbol of the new way of life which is replacing the organized society of Ralph. The hunters have finally made their first kill. Beneath the excitement and jubilation runs an undercurrent of fear at the enormity of the deed. As if to compensate for the fear, there is the beginning of a primitive ritual designed to protect the individual from self-consciousness. The chants and ceremonial ring are like the mask worn by Jack to lose identity. The details of the ritual allow the boys to forget themselves and to become killers.

Notes

bloody - the worst word that Ralph knows, and a word peculiarly offensive to English ears.

dazzle paint - camouflage.

ha'porth - the value of an English halfpenny.

lashings - large amounts.

opalescence - reflections of shimmering rainbow colors.

Character Analyses

Piggy - As civilized as ever, he suggests making a sundial-to keep time in civilized fashion rather than submit to the rhythms of jungle life. While the hair of the other boys becomes long and shaggy as any savages', his remains thin and wispy. The breaking of his glasses stands for partial destruction of his role as intellectual. So far many of his suggestions have been put into effect by Ralph. But as the community becomes more savage, the intellect is further out of place, and Piggy becomes more of an outsider. He is no longer a refining influence but an isolated figure who has lost his relationship to the group.

Jack - When Jack streaks his face with clay, he looks into water at his reflection and is astonished at the change. He dances about, his laughter turning into a bloodthirsty snarl that sends Bill running into the jungle in terror. He discovers that the colors on his face provide a mask behind which he can lose self-consciousness and social inhibitions and become a complete savage. He enjoys the same anonymity as the masked executioner or the masked child at Halloween. The restraining bonds of civilization drop away. He can forget who he is and let his primitive obsession with the hunt take over.

    Roger - possesses a natural appetite for cruelty.

    Maurice - easily led and easily embarrassed.

    Henry - a leader among the littluns.

    Percival - a sickly littlun.

    Johnny - a healthy and naturally belligerent littlun.

LORD OF THE FLIES

TEXTUAL ANALYSIS

CHAPTER 5: BEAST FROM WATER

At the meeting, Ralph gives a lengthy description of the group's failures. He is interrupted by jokes and laughter, and finally Jack leaps up to grab the shell. Ralph makes one last point: there is too much fear on the island. But, though Jack and Piggy agree with Ralph that the fear is groundless, the boys are still disturbed. A littlun comes forward to describe a horrible form that moved in the trees at night. Another, Percival, pushed forward before the assembly, whispers that "the beast comes out of the sea." In the turbulence that follows, Ralph calls for a vote on whether ghosts really exist. The boys vote yes. The meeting ends with the big boys chanting and dancing in a circle while littluns howl.

Comment

For Ralph the island is no longer a storybook kingdom. The dirt on his clothes and body distresses him. His analysis of the ills of the boys is systematic and businesslike. But the nighttime meeting that begins as an attempt to reorganize the lives of the boys creates further chaos. Not only are the boys totally disorganized and more fearful than before, but they seek to forget their fears in savage behavior. The leadership of Ralph, which he sought to strengthen, has deteriorated. At the beginning, the scene on the platform had some semblance of order. Log benches had been carefully arranged before the chief's palace. Ralph was careful to deliver his speech in ABC order. But he cannot handle the fearful boys. His faith in democratic process reaches ludicrous heights as he relies on a majority vote to decide on the authenticity of ghosts. This is the **climax** of a series of futile attempts to legislate fear. If he has learned anything from his experience, he should know that no law can control the turmoil of the human imagination. By the end of the meeting the boys are a howling mob of savages.

In this chapter the darkness of night becomes a symbol of the confused and irrational impulses of the boys. When Piggy and Simon say that the object to fear is inside man, they approach the insight expressed by Joseph Conrad in *Heart of Darkness*, that a darkness existing in man can destroy him if not checked by imagination and reason. Conrad, too, used the jungle setting to represent the dark side of human nature, the mysterious depths of unreason and immorality. This, like Conrad's novel, is a tale of the discovery of the evil powers that lurk beneath the surface of civilized behavior.

Notes

bollocks - testicles.

orgasm - a **climax** of excitement or action.

slug - a slow-moving snail-like bug.

LORD OF THE FLIES

TEXTUAL ANALYSIS

CHAPTER 6: BEAST FROM AIR

While the boys sleep, an explosion lights the sky and a solitary parachute drifts down to the mountain. Sam and Eric, asleep by the signal fire, awaken to see the corpse. They run to tell the others of a strange form that pursued them. In search of the beast, the boys follow Ralph to Castle Rock, a peninsula of stone. The boys have such fun with the boulders and caves of Castle Rock that when Ralph orders them to come to the mountain, they murmur mutinously.

Comment

The power struggle between Ralph and Jack intensifies. Clearly, as the boys move closer to primitive existence and as they recognize the island as their permanent home, Jack emerges as a powerful leader. As long as they see themselves as part of the civilized world with rescue their main objective, Ralph, the sensible one, holds the key to the future.

The likeliest place to hunt the beast is on the mountain where he was sighted. The expedition to the rocky tip of the island seems to be a concession to the fear of the boys, who would prefer to let the signal fire go out rather than to encounter the beast on the mountain. They like the adventure of hunting, but they would prefer to hunt in the relative safety of Castle Rock. And, as the boys avoid the terrors of the jungle, so they refuse to look within themselves for fear of discovering a strange beast.

The dead pilot becomes a representation of the subjective terror of the boys. The pilot's lines are tangled in rock in such a way that his body bobs back and forth. Animation is thus given to the dead form. As Sam and Eric look at the intruder, they see a strange beast, with teeth, claws, and the ability to slink through the trees in pursuit. The grinning death mask, the gloves, and the swinging motion of the pilot are translated, under the influence of fear, into the features and movement of a mysterious creature of destruction. The incident bears out the statements of Piggy and Simon that fear is a human product. The beast is definitely a man, and a most unformidable one-a dead man. The incident also serves as another reminder that the boys on the island are going through their conflicts against a background of war and terror in the larger world. It is ironic that the same emotions of fear and hate should predominate in both, seemingly independent, worlds.

Castle Rock represents the increased primitivism of the boys. It would be an ideal home for barbarians-a natural fortress, with caves to live in and boulders to drop on an enemy below. It invites a way of life far more primitive than that organized by Ralph on the beach. That it should be attractive to the boys indicates their readiness to accept Jack as chief, and live the life of the rock-throwing savage. When a group of boys free a boulder and send it crashing into the sea, we are reminded of the rock that Jack, Simon, and Ralph loosed from the mountain in Chapter 1. These instances of the use of rock as a destructive force are a **foreshadowing** of the murder of Piggy in Chapter 11.

Notes

guano - dung of seafowl.

plinth - a slim ledge of stone projecting like the base of a statue.

waxy - angry.

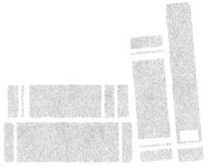

LORD OF THE FLIES

TEXTUAL ANALYSIS

CHAPTER 7: SHADOWS AND SMALL TREES

....

The boys pause in their hunt for the beast to pursue a boar. Ralph joins in. When the boar escapes, the boys chant, "Kill the pig!" and circle about Robert prodding him with their spears in mock murder. Even Ralph feels an urge to tear at the bare flesh. As darkness is falling, Jack challenges Ralph to accompany him to the mountain, Ralph accepts, and Roger joins them. At the top of the cliff, in a gap in the rocks, the three boys see "something like a great ape." It seems at first to be sleeping. But then it lifts a contorted face towards them and they flee in terror.

Comment

The instinct to hunt and destroy a living creature is universal. Ralph has previously failed to recognize this instinct in himself, but now he is driven to behave like a savage. As the behavior of the boys becomes more primitive, the ritual itself increases in significance, with the boys adding a drum and a pretended human victim.

There is a similar lesson concerning the dark side of man in the encounter with the grotesquely twisted corpse on the mountain. The pilot, replacing the signal fire on the mountain, represents the deterioration of human hope. Once he careened across the sky in a plane that represented the apex of human ingenuity and technology. But now he has become less than man-a mere ape-like form. Because his society has used technological discoveries not for the benefit of mankind but for destructive purposes like the development of killer airplanes, the individual is turned into a hunter and killer of other men. Ultimately he is reduced to a sub-human, ape-like condition. The boys, who aspire so highly, with their signal fire a symbol of reason and technology, easily sink to the depths as they become hunters and live, like apes, by instinct instead of by ennobling reason. The boys could see in the ape-like man on the mountain their own images now that all-even Ralph-have succumbed to the pleasures of the hunt. But they fail to read any such lesson.

If Simon were present on this journey, as he was on the first ascent, he would probably solve the mystery of the beast. Unfortunately, he has been replaced by Roger who, by his cruel treatment of the littluns, has identified himself as an instrument of destruction. That it is Roger, and not one of Ralph's followers, who makes the journey indicates the shift in power to the hunters that is taking place.

Notes

dun - dull grayish-brown.

scurfy - flaking or scaling.

traverses - barriers.

windy - afraid.

Character Analyses

Ralph - insecure, as revealed in his falling back into a childhood habit of biting his nails; also, increasingly more prone to dreams of escape.

Simon - mysterious and clairvoyant, he predicts that Ralph will be saved.

LORD OF THE FLIES

TEXTUAL ANALYSIS

CHAPTER 8: GIFT FOR THE DARKNESS

A meeting called to discuss the beast dissolves in fresh conflict between Jack and Ralph. At the suggestion of Piggy, the boys begin to build a signal fire on the beach. But they lose interest and wander off. The author follows Simon into the heart of the jungle where he kneels on the ground. Jack, meanwhile, leads the boys who desert Ralph on a hunt. Surrounding a huge sow, they torment her with their spears until Jack cuts her throat. Simon, who has been sitting nearby, emerges from hiding and gazes at the head of the sow, which the boys have hung on a stick. While Jack and his group are descending on the beach to steal fire for a pig roast, Simon is having a mystical experience. Staring at the pig's head-the Lord of the Flies-he falls into a faint.

Comment

The movement from order to chaos is constantly repeated. The meeting degenerates into a confusion of criticism, bragging and boasting-a covering for the fear and guilt of the boys. The fire that they enthusiastically begin to build on the beach is too large to sustain, so most of the boys simply abandon their responsibility. At the end of the chapter most of the boys have become part of Jack's tribe of hunters. Among those who remain faithful to Ralph, there is a constant yearning for the fun and feasting of the savages that promises a further dissolution. "What makes things break up like they do?" asks Ralph. Piggy blames it on Jack. But a better answer could be found in the evil that exists not only in Jack but in all of the boys in their tendency to destructiveness.

Whenever the author describes the forest cell of Simon, he mentions butterflies that dance in the air. Because of its symmetry and delicate beauty the butterfly has been a traditional representation of airy perfection. Simon is here worshipping the perfect form represented by the butterfly. We are not told whether this perfect form is a completely human ideal, a product of Simon's imagination, or whether it has a divine source. This question Golding wants to leave open.

The attack on the sow is more violent and shocking than the previous slaying of a pig. The boys show remarkable brutality in choosing for destruction the sow with piglets at her dugs-a picture of motherhood and domesticity. The sexual language used to describe the attack, e.g. "The sow collapsed under them and they were heavy and fulfilled upon her," suggests that the boys are fulfilling a primitive unconscious urge to violate their mother. The killing of the sow is the **climax** of the book, the point at which the powers of destruction, embodied by Jack, triumph over the restraints of civilization represented by Ralph. Here the boys totally and irrevocably commit themselves to a savage way of life.

As violent as the description of the killing of the sow appears to be, it should be noticed that Golding controls and checks the imagination of his reader. Instead of following the scene from the point of view of the boys, as he does at the beginning of the **episode**, he backs away and observes the event with detachment. Just before the sow is struck down, he shifts the lens of his camera from close-up to distance, taking in details of the landscape that the eyes of the boys do not observe: "She staggered into an open space where bright flowers grew and butterflies still danced, preoccupied in the centre of the clearing." The butterflies, as a contrast to the violence and brutality, symbolize the quest for pure form that the boys have now completely abandoned, as formlessness and disorder reign uninhibited. The author gives the reader the prerogative of viewing the scene of blood lust and violence with rational detachment.

The head of the sow, hung on a stick as a gift for the beast, becomes another symbol of terror. Golding gives to the head the title "Lord of the Flies," which is a literal translation of the word Beelzebub, the name of a devil in the Bible. The head of the pig represents, however, not so much the evil of sin as the evil of unreason. The flies that buzz over the guts of the sow are mere instinctive beings, and they represent the primitive urges that are beginning to dominate the boys, making them as subject as flies to the influence of the Lord of the Flies. After the hunters panic and run from the head on the stick, Simon encounters it. The Lord of the Flies speaks to Simon, telling him to go away. Simon insists that the Lord of the Flies is no more than a "pig's head on a stick." The **episode** is a symbolic representation of the conflict between the highest and lowest impulses in man. The Lord of the Flies is explaining that there is no sense in trying to hunt and kill the beast. "You knew, didn't you? I'm part of you? Close, close, close! I'm the reason why it's no go? Why things are what they are?" The Lord of the Flies answers the question of why the civilization of the boys is a failure. The destructive element is in the boys themselves-in each boy.

Is the speech of the Lord of the Flies actually of diabolical origin, or is it a figment of Simon's imagination? It could be either. Simon is prone to fits and possesses an active imagination. At the same time, the Lord of the Flies utters truths that are beyond the knowledge of a mere boy in explaining why things are "no go" on the island. In deliberately leaving indefinite the question of the origin of the Lord of the Flies, Golding seems to be saying that it does not matter what name you give to evil, call it devil, sin, neurosis, hate, violence, brutality; the important fact is that evil exists inside man and is a necessary part of the human condition. The symbolic encounter between Simon and the Lord of the Flies represents the conflict between good and evil as it occurs in every man. And just as Simon and the Lord of the Flies represent universal tendencies, so each of the other characters stands for a single quality-cruelty, destructiveness, creativity, or intellect-which exists to a greater or lesser degree in every man. Analyze any individual and you find in him Ralph's tendency to adventure and to common sense, Piggy's intellectualism, Simon's religious and poetic feelings, Roger's willingness to torture, Jack's appetite for destruction, Samneric's desire to please other people. How these different elements are oriented in the individual decides his moral outlook. But they are all present as impulses in the human personality. Thus, at the same time that *Lord of the Flies* is a novel exploring the disintegration of a society, it is also a study of the identity of man.

Notes

do you - take care of you, kill you.

flink - jerk violently.

iridescent - gleaming with the colors of the rainbow.

prefect - a student monitor in charge of discipline in English school.

Character Analyses

Ralph - increasingly more overwrought, his thoughts and speech become disconnected.

Jack - a crybaby when he fails to get his own way, but a formidable hunter and killer when given support. As his hold over the boys strengthens, he increases the forms of savage ritual. Instead of hunting the beast, he tells his followers to hunt pigs and leave a portion of the kill for the beast. This is a placation ceremony-the offering of a part of the kill to the deified beast. While Piggy and Ralph try to impose a mature civilization on the island, one based on their knowledge of the adult world and on their reading, Jack, as if modern civilization never existed, is starting from the beginning and going through the various stages of primitive social development. He begins by establishing an aristocracy of hunters. He evolves a primitive ritual based on primitive fears of originality and self-expression. He instigates a primitive religious worship to feed primitive superstitions. Piggy and Ralph are mistaken in their complete faith in modern society's forms, many of which are ludicrously out of place in the jungle where darkness and disorder reign. On the other hand, to surrender to the forces of darkness, as Jack does, is to surrender one's humanity for a place among the beasts.

LORD OF THE FLIES

TEXTUAL ANALYSIS

CHAPTER 9: A VIEW TO A DEATH

....

Simon awakens and climbs to the top of the mountain. Finding the corpse of the parachutist and freeing its lines, he starts down the mountain. Meanwhile, Ralph, Piggy, and Samneric come to Jack's camp to share the feast of pork. After eating, Jack's hunters begin to dance and shout, "Kill the beast!" Simon stumbles out of the jungle and immediately the group is on him with their pointed sticks. Even Ralph and Piggy join the assault. At this moment, the wind drags the parachute and corpse down the mountain and across the beach into the sea. Then the tide sweeps in, picks up the body of Simon, and carries it away.

Comment

Simon's discovery of the corpse of the parachutist confirms his previous suspicion that the "beast" is an illusion prompted by the imaginations of the boys. But now that he has fathomed the mysteries of the island, will he be heard and believed by the other boys? So far in the novel, the best-informed boys are those least listened to.

Simon does not manage to reveal his discovery. The boys kill him and, with him, all that he represents of imaginative and religious knowledge. Because he understands the nature of evil on the island he is a threat to the continuance of that evil, and so, that evil must destroy him. That all of the boys, including Ralph and Piggy, join in the murderous assault indicates the universality of guilt. The author wants to stress that the potential for such a horrendous crime as the murder of Simon and the contingent destruction of imagination exists in every man.

At the same time that the boys are submitting to evil influences, they are fulfilling a natural desire to deposit all of their guilt in a scapegoat. A scapegoat (originally an actual goat sacrificed to God so that men could escape blame for their sins) is any man, animal, or thing to which is attributed the guilt of a group of people. The boys, feeling guilty about their past failures and crimes, try to lose fear and self-awareness in a ritual act of murder in which Simon becomes a "beast," responsible for the presence of evil on the island. Previously, the pigs were scapegoats through which the boys sought to lose feelings of guilt and inadequacy in the violent act of murder. But, as often happens in unhealthy societies, the first act only increases the need for purgation, and the killings become progressively more criminal, going from pig to sow, and, finally, to a human victim who relieves, momentarily at least, the common guilt. Sir James Frazer, in The Golden Bough, includes an entire chapter on scapegoats, describing the scores of ways that primitive tribes ceremonially deposit their guilt on a single object, animal, or person and then proceed to harm or destroy the guilt laden creature. Often, the primitive tribes will use sticks to beat the scapegoat, as the boys do.

The significance of the vanishing of the parachute and corpse into the sea at the moment of Simon's death is that now the beast on top of the mountain is no longer necessary. His place is to be supplied by human beasts. It is ironic that Simon, who hoped to dispel the beast by enlightening the boys, instead replaces the beast as the imagined source of evil. After Simon, the savage society will turn its violence against Piggy, and then Ralph.

Notes

bourdon - a droning sound like the wail of the bagpipe.

phosphorescence - a glowing in the dark.

LORD OF THE FLIES

TEXTUAL ANALYSIS

CHAPTER 10: THE SHELL AND THE GLASSES

Piggy and Ralph, conscience stricken at their participation in the murder of Simon, are near hysteria. Meanwhile, all of the biguns except Piggy, Ralph, and Samneric have moved out onto the rocky tip of the island, Castle Rock. On the cliff above the ledge that leads to Castle Rock, a boulder is poised, ready to crush any intruder. While Ralph and Piggy are preparing for sleep, Jack and two followers attack them to steal fire. After a vicious fight, Jack runs off carrying Piggy's broken glasses.

Comment

Although Jack and his followers pretend that their victim was an unknown beast, they are obviously so guilt ridden after the murder of Simon that they try to drown their consciences in new violence. Without cause, Jack beats one of the boys. He has a rock poised on the cliff-a symbol of his mortal hatred for Ralph and Piggy.

The stealing of Piggy's glasses represents the complete defeat of the intellectual by the savage. Now Ralph, who has been relying more and more on Piggy in recent chapters, has, for all practical purposes, lost his brain trust, and Jack rules as the absolute monarch of the island domain.

The sand castles of Chapter 4 have been destroyed and with them the romantic adventure and hopefulness of youth. Here the scene is a castle of rock, a natural home for a primitive cave man. Jack and his followers have become creatures of instinct. Both civilized forms and romantic dreams have been replaced by the law of survival of the fittest. All hopes for the rescue of the group and the return to civilization are swallowed in a wave of destructive passion. Kill or be killed becomes the motto of the group of boys whose hearts have turned as hard as Castle Rock.

Notes

round the bend - crazy.

bomb happy - deranged, as by the constant pressure of warfare.

Character Analysis

Ralph-less and less a competent leader. Awake, he is distracted by daydreams; asleep, he is disturbed by nightmares.

LORD OF THE FLIES

TEXTUAL ANALYSIS

CHAPTER 11: CASTLE ROCK

That morning, the fire having gone out, Ralph blows the conch and calls an assembly, but only Piggy, the twins and a scattering of littluns attend. They go to Castle Rock and confront Jack, who answers Ralph's criticism by lunging at him with his spear. Jack orders his savages to tie the twins. When Ralph and Jack begin to fight, Piggy calls for attention. But Roger releases a boulder from above that smashes into Piggy, flinging his body into the sea. Ralph eludes the spears of the hunters and leaps into the jungle. Samneric are tortured by Jack and Roger until they agree to join the tribe.

Comment

In Chapter 4, Roger, restrained by habits of civilized behavior, could not throw stones directly at a human being. Early in this chapter, as Roger removes his hands from the log under the boulder above the entrance to Castle Rock, in order to throw stones at the twins, Golding makes the comment that "Some source of power began to pulse in Roger's body." The power is now stronger than any habitual restraint. It is the destructive power of prehistoric man who kills his victims with primitive weapons. When Ralph shouts at Jack, "Which is better, laws and rescue, or hunting and breaking things up?" he summarizes the conflicts in the book between the ideals of modern society and the impulses of primitive man. Roger provides an answer first in the stones that he throws at Piggy, then in the huge boulder. He and Jack have become complete savages.

When Piggy is thrown into the sea, he lands first on a red rock, then is swept away by the retreating sea. The red rock is like an altar on which Piggy is sacrificed to the forces of destruction represented in the stones and boulder of Roger, and in the motion of the all-consuming sea. The event symbolizes the obliteration of intellect and reason from the island. After the most exalted flowering of society in the ideals of religion and poetry is destroyed with the death of Simon, the intellectual forms of society, the highly developed laws of social intercourse, are killed. The experience on the island is the story of human civilization in reverse. The smashing of the conch shell at the moment of Piggy's death represents the loss of the traditional systems of authority so cherished by Piggy. It is appropriate that the sea, which Triton controlled by blowing his conch, should rear up and snatch Piggy after the conch is shattered.

Notes

myopia - nearsightedness,

truculently - fiercely.

Character Analyses

Piggy - achieves a greater dignity before his death by the determination with which he goes to meet Jack to speak his piece.

Roger - Although he feels the "hangman's horror," the tremendous burden of guilt borne by one whose task is to extinguish human life cold-bloodedly, he achieves greater strength and forcefulness as he becomes a master of torture, cruelty, and destruction.

LORD OF THE FLIES

TEXTUAL ANALYSIS

CHAPTER 12: CRY OF THE HUNTERS

Later in the day, Ralph, bloody and weary, encounters the skull of the pig, the Lord of the Flies, and strikes out at it. Dodging in and out of the jungle, he continues to elude his pursuers, who have accidentally started a forest fire. Just as Ralph is about to be caught, a British naval officer appears. He thinks that he has interrupted a game until Ralph informs him that two boys have been killed. The officer asks who is boss, and Ralph asserts that he is. How is it, the officer asks in shocked disbelief, that a "pack of British boys" couldn't have "put up a better show?"

Comment

When Ralph encounters the Lord of the Flies, he goes through an experience similar to Simon's before his death. Though he knocks over the pig's skull, it keeps grinning at him, as if to remind him that it is a part of him, just as it was of Simon, and just as it is of all of the boys. Jack, Simon, and Ralph may be very different types, but they are alike in their proneness to evil. Though Ralph and Simon try to ignore the destructive force within themselves, and Jack tries to submerge his good impulses, each boy is a battleground where the forces of corruption wage war on the forces of good. Each boy is a mixture of good and evil. When Samneric confide to Ralph that Roger has sharpened a stick at both ends to use for him, they reveal the extent of the debasement of the boys. Ralph apparently is to be treated like the sow, his head stuck in the ground on a stick sharpened at both ends, his body cooked and eaten by the cannibalistic boys. When Ralph himself, to avoid detection, relies on cunning like that of the pig, he reveals how easy it is for a human to slip into the role of beast.

The officer, pompous, precise, proud of his clothes and trim cutter, suffers from the same moral blindness that Ralph did early in the book. On the other hand, wearing a gun and commanding a gun boat, he possesses a power of destruction like Jack's. He too, in spite of his dignity and fondness for a "good show," is a hunter who fails to recognize the vileness of his career. And though he is, like the primitive hunters on the island, obsolete in a future world of atomic warfare and supersonic air travel, he is a symbol of the chain of destruction present on the island and continuous in the "civilized" world. At the end, Ralph is crying "for the end of innocence, the darkness of man's heart, and the fall through the air of the true, wise friend called Piggy." The officer, embarrassed, turns away. This is no way for British boys to carry on. The officer's ideas about British boys are as out-of-date as his weapons. He is a throwback to the days when England was still Queen of the Seas, and when such a title had some importance.

Ralph's phrase, "the darkness of man's heart," is an **allusion** to Conrad's *Heart of Darkness* where a similar concept of self-recognition is expressed. In every man, according to Conrad, there is a darkness that he must discover. Either he sees and controls this dark presence, or it dominates him. To ignore the fact of evil is to destroy all possibility of learning from it. This **theme** of Conrad's becomes the lesson represented in the boys' experience on the island.

At the end of the novel the entire island is scorched by fire- another example of the irresponsibility of the boys. The island, more than ever, resembles a city consumed by atomic warfare.

Notes

diddle - trick.

pax - Latin for peace, a guarantee of free passage in children's games.

ratings - enlisted men.

Character Analyses

Ralph - at the end, a boy again, weeping, but mature in his knowledge of the loss of innocence.

Jack - a "little boy" at the end, standing in the background while Ralph speaks for the group to the naval officer.

Officer - possesses the pretension, pride, and destructiveness that have ruined the society of the boys and that ruin the society of civilized man.

LORD OF THE FLIES

CHARACTER ANALYSES

Ralph

An attractive boy and a natural leader, the sort of intelligent, well-adjusted, athletic boy who easily might become the idol of his schoolmates. We meet him in the first chapter as he leads the way out of the jungle while Piggy lumbers after him. That he is fair-haired suggests that he is a child of fortune, one who is blessed by nature with grace, strength, and luck. There is recklessness to his manner. He seems happy at the prospect of living on a deserted island, away from the influence of adults. The setting fosters dreams of heroic adventure in which he is the **protagonist**. He will overcome all of the difficulties present in his surroundings, lead a joyously exciting jungle life, then optimistically await a glamorous rescue by his naval-officer father. Unfortunately, his dreams are frustrated when nature and his fellow youths refuse to cooperate with his romantic vision. And, as his dream becomes more difficult of attainment, he loses confidence and calmness and begins to indulge himself in escape fantasies and dreams of the past. Gradually, he forfeits the respect of the other boys. A contrasting characteristic to his tendency to dream is his common sense. He is quick to assess the situation of the boys in realistic terms. He sees what must be done for their survival and rescue and sets about arranging parliamentary meetings, building a signal fire, and constructing huts. He appraises the advice of Piggy according to its practicality. He fights against the superstition and terror of the boys as being detrimental to the organized progress of their society. Ralph is by no means a perfect character. He is often mean to those weaker than himself, particularly the faithful Piggy. Occasionally he performs rash and foolish actions. He even joins in the murder of Simon. He shares in the universal guilt of man. But he does show a clear sightedness that none of the others possess in the same way. It is his common-sense view that prevails at the end of the novel when he graduates from his experience on the island with a more mature knowledge of himself and the world around him. He recognizes the universal presence of evil as a condition of life. He is capable of appreciating the tragedy of the loss of innocence that is the common heritage of man.

More than any other character, Ralph represents the outlook of the author-and the outlook that he expects his reader to share. He is not as intellectual as Piggy and he is not as religious as Simon, but he dreams the dreams of freedom and adventure that enliven the progress of western society. He is the most complete, most human, and most heroic of the characters in the novel, and the one with whom readers most readily identify.

Jack Merridew

"He was tall, thin, and bony, and his hair was red beneath the black cap. His face was crumpled and freckled, and ugly without silliness." A cruel and ugly bully, he early develops a taste for violence. He is a leader of the choir at first, and then of the hunters. His leadership resides in his ability to threaten and frighten those under him. He is always ready for a fight. His victory over Piggy represents the triumph of violence over intellect, as he smashes one of the lenses of the fat boy's glasses. The knife that he carries is a symbol of the death and destruction that accompany his every act. He does have some attractive qualities-bravery and resourcefulness. But these are easily obscured by his wrath, envy, pride, hatred, and lust for blood. He is constantly attempting to weaken Ralph's hold on the boys. He suggests opposite measures, he shouts abusively, he threatens, he is constantly demanding to be made chief. In all, he is a complete stranger to polite behavior. In his constant rivalry with Ralph, and in his constant preoccupation with killing, whether it be pigs or fellow human beings, he is a diabolical force, plunging the boys into a chaos of brute activities. His egotistical outbursts and his temper tantrums suggest that he is immature in his social development. But as hunter and killer he is extremely precocious. The readiness with which he throws himself into the existence of a savage, as he pauses to sniff the air for scent, or falls to his knees to inspect the pig droppings, or runs naked and painted through the forest, suggests the flimsiness of the restraints and patterns of civilization in a personality in which the destructive passions flow strongly.

If the novel is read as religious allegory, Jack emerges as an envoy of the Devil, enticing the other boys to sin. If the novel is read as a representation of Freudian principles, Jack represents the primitive urges of the id. In the symbolic representation of the processes of life and death, Jack suggests, both in the black cloaks which he and his followers wear and in his association with darkness, the power of death. In his first appearance, coming out of the "darkness of the forest" to face Ralph, whom he cannot see because his back is to the sun, Jack represents the Satanic and deathly force coming to confront the divine and life giving man of light. The blood that he wallows in is a further representation of deathliness. When, after his first kill, "Jack transferred the knife to his left hand and smudged blood over his forehead as he pushed down the plastered hair," he unconsciously imitates the ritual of the tribal initiation of the hunter, whose face is covered with the blood of his first kill. Finally, if the novel is read as the story of human civilization, Jack represents the influences of unreason and confusion and violence as they operate counter to the progress of human virtues and social institutions.

Piggy

This intellectual is an outsider. He manages for a time to have some influence on the group through Ralph, who recognizes his brilliance and puts into effect several of his suggestions. But, generally, the boys are quick to ridicule him for his fatness, asthma, and lack of physical skill. An orphan brought up under the care of an aunt, he has developed into a sissy. He cannot do anything for himself, whether it be to gather fruit, blow the conch shell, or build huts. He always tries to hide when the other boys are involved in manual labor. At home, presumably, his favorite pastime would be sitting in a chair, reading. His frequent appeals to the adult world, and his attempt to model his behavior on that of teachers and other grown-ups evokes the contempt of the boys. Further, he makes the mistake of pressing too hard for acceptance. In his first appearance in Chapter 1, he attempts so diligently to win the favor or Ralph that he only alienates Ralph at the same time that he gives him personal information about himself that Ralph can then use to hurt him. His life on the island is a series of unhappy embarrassments, including being taunted by the boys, being beaten, and having his glasses broken and stolen. Finally, at the instigation of Jack, he is killed by Roger.

He represents an attitude of mind that is conservative and civilized. His eyeglasses, which are constantly steamed, and that he absolutely needs to see anything, separate him from the world of activity and adventure in which he cannot participate as freely as the other boys, and confine him to the realm of his own mind. Possibly because he is the bookish member of the group, he tends to be more scientific than the rest, and also more skeptical. His knowledge of science is shown in his plan to build sundials. His skepticism keeps him from participating in the superstitions of the other boys. He knows that the world of adults and books would not abide the legend of the "beastie."

Piggy is necessarily more civilized than anyone else because, with his meagre physical equipment, only in the most civilized of societies could he survive. Ironically, with his build, his nickname "Piggy," and his squealing, he resembles the sacrificial pig. When he dies, his "arms and legs twitched a bit, like a pig's after it has been killed." His superior intellect is of little use to him in the later stages of the novel. In the increasingly more degenerate society of the boys, the intellectual is lowered to the status of the beast. Then he is sacrificed and symbolically eaten.

Simon

An artistically and religiously sensitive boy who looks, without blinking, into the evil realities that plague the island. In spite of his delicate frame and frequent fainting spells, he is willing to work and is brave in the face of physical danger. At the same time, he seems to be something of a mystic, stealing off into the depths of the jungle for moments of solitude and meditation. Perhaps it is his belief in spiritual reality that diminishes his fear of death and his attachment to the things of the world. He works at building the huts, and is happy to gather fruit for the littluns without any selfish motives. He enters the dark forest without any fear of strange "beasts." He does not share the fears of the other boys because he feels that the spirit world does not hold any terrors.

He is right in saying that the only "beasts" are the ones that people create. He is perhaps wrong in underestimating this evil, even though it is a subjective one. He discovers, in his conversation with the Lord of the Flies, that even he himself contains a destructive evil. And he discovers at the cost of his life the full power of the evil that throbs in the hearts of the boys. After solving the mystery of the "beast" by discovering the dead parachutist on the mountain, he is rewarded by being beaten and stabbed to death by the horde of maniacal boys.

It is in terms of the religious meaning of the story that Simon is most important. He represents the idea that, even in the most unattached and spiritual personality, an evil presence makes itself known. On the social level, he represents a creative force that is cut off from the rest of society because of the predominance of violent impulses in that society.

On the historical level, Simon represents the gradual alienation of the creative artist, in this century, as he is forced further and further into a position of isolation until he climbs so high in his ivory tower that he can commune only with the spirits.

Roger

A furtive, quiet boy, who evolves into a torturer and terrorist, eager to throw rocks, or roll boulders, or prod his fellow man with spears. He represents a different kind of destructiveness than that of Jack. Where Jack acts in fury, Roger performs his treacheries with cool detachment. He appears to know full well the evil of his actions, but not really to care. He actually enjoys being called upon to play the role of torturer. It is such perversity that makes him much more evil in the mind of the reader. Whereas Simon joined Jack and Ralph on their ascent of the mountain because of his spiritual confidence. Roger willingly joins Jack and Ralph in search of the "beast," because he is so conversant with the realm of evil that he fears nothing. His own diabolism is his security from evil mishap.

In terms of the historical and social allegory, Roger is the professional exterminator of human beings that usually is found in the entourage of a tyrant. On the religious level, Roger represents the complete death of conscience; he is the epitome of evil. In the Freudian myth he represents, even more explicitly than does Jack, the force of the id. In connection with the **imagery** of life and death, he suggests and absolute lust for death.

Samneric

Sam and Eric, identical twins, are extremely civilized, possibly because since birth they have been a small, two-man society. They are shy and pleasant. It is the twins who spot the corpse of the parachutist on the top of the mountain and run in panic to report a beast. They are not especially brave, but they remain faithful to Ralph long after the others. In their cheery comradeship they represent the best of the English schoolboy tradition. That Jack and Roger are able, at the end, to make them serve as hunters and to betray Ralph is an indication of the power of evil on the island that even they must share in it. They resemble the relatively innocent and humane members of civilized society who are forced to submit to the powers of mechanization, and sacrifice their personalities to become part of a process of destruction.

Maurice

Although good-natured and smiling, he is easily swayed by the evil influence of Roger and Jack. He possesses qualities of pleasantness and affability, and would be a happy member of a civilized community. But on the island he is forced to bend before the will of the hunters.

Henry

A leader among the littluns. Golding seems to be pointing out that even in the smallest and least significant units of society there are the same combinations of leaders and followers with all of the attendant duties and rights. It is Henry whom Roger follows in Chapter 4, in order to throw stones in his direction.

Percival

A small, sickly, and fearful littlun. He reports that he saw the beast, and that the beast came out of the sea.

Johnny

A healthy and naturally belligerent littlun.

British Officer

The only character from the adult world is proud, pretentious, and blind to the faults of his society-just as the boys are blind to theirs. Though he represents the authority that the boys have shown they needed on the island, he also symbolizes the weakness, destructiveness, and hypocrisy of the society from which he comes.

LORD OF THE FLIES

ESSAY QUESTIONS AND ANSWERS

THE IDEAS OF GOLDING

Question: What is the **theme** of *Lord of the Flies*?

Answer: **Theme**, as a critical term, refers both to the truth about human life, which an author wants to emphasize in a piece of fiction, and to the idea that controls the climactic action in a story. In *Lord of the Flies* the **theme** is that evil is present as a destructive influence in man, operating counter to the forces of reason and civilization. This idea is not only revealed in several scenes where the boys perform destructive acts. It is present as the reason why things happen the way they do in the central portion of the novel, where the forces of Jack triumph over the forces of Ralph. It is present in the brutal destruction of the sow, in the ritual sacrifice of Simon, and in the wanton murder of Piggy. It is the truth about human life that one is forced to accept as an explanation of the destruction of the society of the boys.

Question: According to Golding, what are the limitations of the boys?

Answer: Not only are the boys frustrated in their attempt to establish an island society because of their evil natures. They also lack the traditional restraints of society that can sometimes control evil; for example, a coherent religious code, or an effective legal code. They are also too immature to harmonize their various differing members into a functional whole. They lack the self-control, perseverance, and cooperativeness necessary to the development of any social organism, whether it be a basketball team or the United Nations.

Question: What is Golding's opinion of modern society?

Answer: The parallels between the society of the boys and modern civilized society, such as the competitiveness, destructiveness, and violence existing in both, suggest that the problems that plague the boys are those that are present in more sophisticated communities. There is the same proneness to evil, the same fear of the unknown, the same use of technology for inhuman purposes. At the same time, there is the same potential for civilized advancement, provided that human reason is allowed to flourish in company with, but not stifled by, a strong moral sense.

Question: What is the author's attitude to history?

Answer: History is a record of ironic recurrences of human error. The same errors that were made by primitive man are made by the boys, and are made by civilized societies, even to the point where human sacrifices are still being offered to appease the gods of terror and fear. Golding seems to be pointing out that the blood lust of the primitive hunter is prevalent in modern man, as witness his warships, bombers, and rockets.

Question: What does Golding say about human destiny?

Answer: At first glance, the future seems gray. Society is disintegrating. Anarchy and violence thrive at the expense of reason. At the end of *Lord of the Flies*, however, there is some hope for the future in the new knowledge that Ralph has acquired. He understands the conflict of good and evil, ideal and real, that exists in man. And, unlike Simon and Piggy, he is resourceful enough to elude death and to carry this knowledge back to civilization, there to have some influence of his fellow man. He will be a wise leader when he is a man. He will be a man of reason, but also a man aware of the darkness lurking in the most innocent person. And he will have some positive effect on civilization.

Question: What is the ethical view expressed in *Lord of the Flies*?

Answer: Ethics, in this novel, are complex. The good man is not necessarily one who intends to perform good actions. He is certainly not one who accepts the mores of a society, because the mores on the island include murder and torture. Rather, he is the person who works for his fellow man, who answers the dictates of reason, who accepts a personal responsibility for the evil in the world, and is able to function as a harmonious human being. Simon is perhaps the most holy person in the novel, but he does not function effectively in society. Ralph, the leader who best coordinates his activities, is the most ethical character.

Question: What is Golding's concept of a hero?

Answer: Conventional heroic types like the dashing naval captain are satirized. The hero is the leader who works for the creation and advancement of society, who recognizes and challenges the evil existing in himself, and who is capable of enduring in a complex and often savage environment.

Question: What is the significance of the title?

Answer: The title, Lord of the Flies, is a reminder for the reader of who it is that the boys are submitting to as they become more savage and superstitious. The expression is a translation of Beelzebub, the name of a devil, which suggests that the boys are becoming more evil as they establish the Lord of the Flies on a stick, and begin to worship the mysterious forces of the jungle. Further, the title suggests that the boys are like flies, mere instinctive beings swarming to the kill.

Question: What is the meaning of Simon's encounter with the Lord of the Flies?

Answer: Simon, who represents the highest aspirations of the human spirit towards beauty and holiness, participates in a symbolic dialogue with the Lord of the Flies, who represents the lowest part of man, the source of violence, hatred, fear, murder. The meeting represents the recognition of these forces in all men, even the saintly. The **episode** refutes benevolent and optimistic theories of man and the universe.

Question: What is the meaning of fire?

Answer: In the novel, fire represents a hope for the future. Fire has distinguished man from the beasts for as long as he has been building fires for cooking and warmth. Here, the fire denotes a peculiarly human action, the use of a signal to win the aid of fellow men. As long as the signal fire is lit, the boys are confident of their place in the community of civilized people. Fire is a contrast to the symbol of darkness that represents the barbarism within the boys.

Question: Explain the meaning of the hunt.

Answer: The hunt is a formalization of the destructive passions that exist in the boys. It gives these passions an outlet. This, however, is dangerous because the more these passions are indulged, the more violent they become.

Question: What is the significance of the corpse and the parachute on the mountain?

Answer: The corpse and parachute are evidence of the subjective nature of human fear. Distorted by the imaginations of the boys, these harmless objects become so frightening that the signal fire is allowed to go out. They are an illustration that man has nothing to fear but himself.

Question: What is the relation of the individual to the state according to Golding?

Answer: Each individual should contribute to the total harmonious operation of society.

Question: What is man's relation to nature?

Answer: Nature "red in tooth and claw" represents a threat to man, unless, by the use of reason, he understands and controls its powers.

Question: Comment on the importance of self-discovery in the novel.

Answer: It is only insofar as a character knows himself that he can do anything to improve conditions in the novel. All of the attempts to civilize the island, to erect huts, to organize a parliament, to sustain a signal fire, fail because of not allowing for the limitations of the boys. It is only at the end of the novel, when Ralph recognizes the loss of his own innocence, that knowledge paves the way for progress.

Question: To what extent is man free according to Golding?

Answer: Freedom is always qualified by forces inside and outside of man. Society imposes restrictions on the freedom of man and these may be the helpful rules that Ralph establishes, or they may be the rites of a savage tribe that Samneric are forced to conform to. But even more strongly, the dark side of man controls his desires and actions and limits his powers of choice. It is only as man recognizes the threat to his liberty, without and within, that he can begin to define his rights as a free being and proceed to control his destiny. Freedom is dependent upon self-knowledge.

THE FORM OF LORD OF THE FLIES

Question: Discuss Golding's handling of point of view.

Answer: In this novel Golding uses the omniscient author point of view, permitting his to enter any mind. However, he often presents his material with cool objectivity. He does not let his reader involve himself completely with his own, or his characters' feelings. His tone in cool and analytical. Even in the most violent scenes, he will detachedly observe butterflies at the same time that he presents the central action. He seems to be encouraging his reader to decide on the issues with calmness and reason, the same qualities that the author himself exhibits as he narrates the story.

Question: Analyze the use of symbolism in the novel.

Answer: The author gives to almost every detail in the story a meaning of its own and a representational meaning in terms of the **theme** of the development of evil on the island. The boys themselves are representative of different ways of life-the intellectual, the adventurer, the bully, the torturer-so as to give the impression of diversity that is found in an actual society. The places represent human potentials; for example, the jungle the darkness of the human spirit, the sea the destructiveness of man, the platform reason, the mountain hope. Objects like the boulder and Jack's knife represent powers of violence inside the boys. The conch shell stands for order and stability. Incidents, for example the several hunting rituals, symbolize the increasing powers of evil.

Question: Is Golding in any sense a realistic writer?

Answer: He seems less interested in the reality of external events than in spiritual and moral reality. Although he writes concretely, the experiences are not likely to ever actually occur. He is realistic in the presentation of the psychology of violence. His projections of the impulses to hunt and destroy, as they exist in modern man, are based on accurate interpretation.

Question: What is the structure of *Lord of the Flies*?

Answer: The general organization of the novel is chronological order, with a concentration on the successive by the boys to organize their lives on the island and the successive attempts failures. The novel moves from hope to frustration to hope to frustration-with each new hope dimmer and each frustration greater as the society disintegrates into a state of anarchy.

Question: What is the advantage of using boys as characters?

Answer: The boys, with their outward innocence and inner corruption, represent, quite readily, the **theme** of the intrusion of evil in man. Much of the **irony** in the novel derives from the discrepancy between pleasant appearances and horrible realities. Even the relatively civilized boys, Piggy and Ralph, join in the slaughter of their friend Simon.

Question: What are the methods of characterization?

Answer: Golding uses the conventional methods of revealing character, presenting the thoughts, speech, and description of a person, describing characteristic action, and reporting the observations of others; all of these are used with great economy. The boys are created with a few deft strokes, rather than by a multiplicity of details, with the result that all of the boys, except perhaps Simon and Ralph, are simple characterizations. This makes them serve better as representative types in the symbolic narrative. Even with Simon and Ralph, Golding gives greatest emphasis to one characteristic of Simon-his spiritualism-and two characteristics of Ralph-his dreaminess and his common sense-to make each of them also symbolize a way of life.

Question: Do the characters of the boys develop?

Answer: The personalities of the boys do change. In general, there is the gradual flowering of evil that warps their characters. In some boys there is a change for the better. Piggy at the end is more dignified. Simon is filled with an adult wisdom. Ralph is serious and sombre.

Question: Comment on style and tone.

Answer: Golding writes with great virtuosity. At times he describes the details of the jungle so concretely and vividly that the reader is convinced of the reality of the experience. Other times he lyrically presents the imaginative experience of the boys, as in Chapter 4 where he depicts the illusions that beset the boys, or in Chapter 8 where he brings Simon face-to-face with the Lord of the Flies. His tone ranges from a romantically enthusiastic response to the beauty of the jungle, to a satiric juxtaposition of incongruous elements like the childish chatter and vicious expressions of hatred by the boys.

Question: How does the author sustain interest?

Answer: It is the physical, emotional, and moral conflicts of boy against boy, and boy against nature that arouse and sustain interest.

Question: What is the advantage of using an island setting?

Answer: The island is a completely isolated world, where the possibility of instituting a new society can be tested. The island, too, will take whatever geography the author wants to impose. Here, Golding molds the island to his symbolic purposes, giving it a beach, platform, jungle, mountain, and rocky extremity, each of which can be used to represent human potentials and aspirations.

THE INHERITORS

TEXTUAL ANALYSIS

CHAPTER I

A group of eight primitive people migrating to the mountains to their summer camping grounds are thrown into panic when they discover that the log by which they habitually cross a river is missing. Their Leader, Mal, advises them to lay another log on the water, and they all manage to cross, although Mal falls in the water.

Comment

Homo neanderthalensis, parts of whose skeleton were found in the Neanderthal, a valley of the Rhine River, is said to be the extinct predecessor of the human species, Homo sapiens. In an epigraph, Golding quotes from H. G. Wells's description, in *Outline of History*, of the Neanderthal man as gorilla-like, with "an extreme hairiness, an ugliness, or a repulsive strangeness in his appearance over and above his low forehead, his beetle brows, his ape neck, and his inferior stature...." Golding's Neanderthal is a primitive creature, capable only of the most rudimentary thought, who operates in imitation of remembered pictures rather than according to logic. For example, Mal remembers from long ago the floating of a log on water, and so is capable of repeating the action. But he has no sense of the rational use of materials to meet new ends. When these characters refer to their mind's processes, they say, "I have a picture," instead of "I think." This is to indicate a primitive mentality that deals in sensations, feelings, and visual memories rather than in concepts of cause and effect.

But, in contrast to Wells's view of Neanderthal man as a completely brutish creature, Golding suggests that, in terms of his spiritual sensitivity, the Neanderthal is superior to modern man. He sees a river and reacts in terror because he perceives a spirit in the river. When the tribe come to their camping grounds, they see, on the mountain above, ice formations resembling the form of a woman, and they begin to cry out to the goddess Oa. The chapter ends with a lyrical description of the ritual of the new fire as the old woman breathes life into a lump of clay. Her words conclude the chapter: "The fire is awake again." For this tribe of primitive men, the world is full of souls.

THE INHERITORS

TEXTUAL ANALYSIS

CHAPTER II

....

Gathered together in their cave, the members of the group listen while the mortally ill Mal speaks of his past memories and then assigns the duties of gathering wood and hunting. We follow the movements of Lok, who has been sent out to find food.

Comment

In spite of its primitiveness, this group shares some of the qualities of modern society. It has an organization of parts as, under the leadership of Mal, some are designated as hunters and others as wood gatherers. The care of children is divided among the women. Members are bound by ties of loyalty and feeling, such as the tenderness expressed for children and for the aged. And they feel for their home - the cave - a love born of familiar associations of sight and smell. In addition, the tribe has a religion that goes beyond the personification of water and fire to the worship of a personal deity, Oa, who "brought forth the earth from her belly." And there is a religious legend, resembling the story of the Garden of Eden in Genesis, of the time "when it was summer all year round and the flowers and fruit hung on the same branch." All of these elements, as well as the bewilderment of these creatures living in a time in which their world of natural plenty is undergoing frightful changes and their society is disintegrating, should help to make the primitive group sympathetic and understandable to the modern reader.

Characters

The eight characters are, as we later learn, the last survivors of a Neanderthal tribe depleted by forest fire. In general, they have the, intellectual development of children a few years old. Golding gives them extremely simple names to signify that their new language is undeveloped.

Mal: The aged leader who is dying after falling into the water. His mind is stocked with a lifetime of memories of the activities of the tribe as well as a genealogy of its leaders as far back as Oa. At times, his mind seems to be approaching rational thought.

The Old Woman: Presumably the wife of Mal, although family relationships are loosely defined in this primitive group. A creature of dignity and spiritual wisdom, she tends the sick and is the priestess in religious ritual.

Ha: Responsible and heroic, the second in command. It is Ha who manages to drag the log across the river and it is he who pulls Mal from the water.

Nil: A nursing mother, probably Ha's mate.

Lok: An attractive but flighty young man. Although Golding uses the omniscient author point of view, he tends to rely on Lok's outlook. And, as the story progresses, Lok becomes a more sensitive and serious protagonist.

Fa: A mate of Lok's; she cares for Nil's baby.

Liku: A young girl who carries a doll-like replica of the goddess Oa. She rides on the shoulders of Lok, whose affection for her rivals his love for Fa.

The New One: Nil's baby boy.

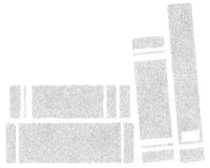

THE INHERITORS

TEXTUAL ANALYSIS

CHAPTER III

Fa, Lok, and Liku, searching for food, come upon a carcass of a doe surrounded by hyenas. They fight off the hyenas and bring the doe to the camp. But the joy of the feast is broken when Nil, who has been gathering wood with Ha, returns and reveals that Ha is lost. When she last saw him, he seemed to be smiling at someone at the edge of the river. When she came to the river, she found the scent of another man.

Comment

When they fight the hyenas, Fa and Lok use sticks and stones. Their tactics are as limited as their animal movements as they barely manage to outwit the hyenas. They are certainly no match for whatever dark agency has removed their log from the river and has spirited off Ha.

With the loss of Ha, the organization of the little group is broken. The second in command, the heir to Mal, who is ill, Ha is probably the most essential member of the group. Lok is obviously too immature to assume leadership.

The gentleness of the Neanderthal people is stressed in this chapter. They respect all of nature as coming from the womb of Oa and, accordingly, will not kill to eat although they will eat what is already dead.

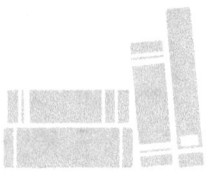

THE INHERITORS

TEXTUAL ANALYSIS

CHAPTER IV

....

The old woman sends Lok to search for Ha. At the edge of the river he calls out and as a strange cry is heard coming from an island in the river, a human form appears. Two rituals are described in the chapter. The first is a prayer offering by Lok and Fa to Oa in the caves of ice. The second is the ceremony accompanying Mal's death.

Comment

This remnant of prehistoric society is endangered from within and without. Mal, perhaps because of his years, has miscalculated the seasons and brought his people too early to their summer home, and so they must bear a cold climate. And now, with his death, the group is without a leader. Ha is missing. We later learn that the Neanderthals are being preyed upon by a tribe of Homo sapiens, the progenitors of modern man. Lok, although a strong and able hunter, cannot distinguish between the "pictures" in his memory and actual events. Therefore the old woman directs the group.

The tribe, a naturally joyous people given to games and laughter, has a healthy attitude toward death. The old man, Mal, realizing that his time has come, calmly asks to be laid in the warm earth. They lay him in fetal position in Oa's womb - the earth. There is a modest eulogy in the old woman's words: "When Mal was strong he found much food." There is a suggestion of a belief in an afterlife in the placing of water and a haunch of meat in the grave and in the ritual formula: "Eat, Mal, when you are hungry," and "Drink, Mal, when you are thirsty."

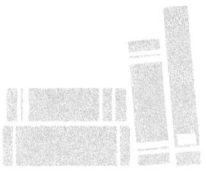

THE INHERITORS

TEXTUAL ANALYSIS

CHAPTER V

....

Lok, again looking for Ha, sees a fire on the island and shouts across, but the new people run for cover. Then he hears the cries of Liku as she is carried across the river. As he runs up and down screaming for Liku, a strange face appears on the island shore and shoots a feathered stick at him. Crawling out on a branch over the water, Lok looks down and sees the body of the old woman.

Comment

There is much dramatic irony in this chapter as Golding describes events as they appear to the limited mind of Lok. It is for the reader to put events into a context of cause and effect. When the man on the island shoots the arrow, Lok, never having seen bow or arrow, mistakes it for a token of friendship. The reader, however, is able to appreciate from the details that this is a poisoned arrow, that the strange face, different from Lok's because it has forehead and chin, is that of a human being, and that the superiority of the new people to the Neanderthals in weaponry will lead to the destruction of the primitive tribe. The abduction of Liku and the drowning of the old woman are similar events by which Lok can only be baffled but which the reader can see as part of an over-all pattern. Golding's description of the old woman floating under the water is characteristic of his technique of objective - but evocative - reporting: "She was ignoring the injuries to her body, her mouth was open, the tongue showing and the specks of dirt were circling slowly in and out as though it had been nothing but a hole in a stone. Her eyes swept across the bushes, across his face, looked through him without seeing him, rolled away and were gone."

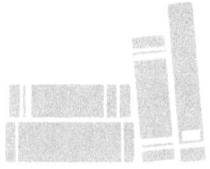

THE INHERITORS

TEXTUAL ANALYSIS

CHAPTER VI

Returning to a deserted camp, Lok learns from Fa, who has been hiding, that the new people have killed Nil and the old woman and taken Nil's baby away. They see two men cross the river in a log - the first canoe they have ever seen - and they find logs themselves and make their way to the island camp of the new people where a man wearing a stag's head is dancing. When Lok shouts for Liku, the new people pursue him.

Comment

The Neanderthals, a naturally friendly people, quickly learn to associate danger with the new people, a ruthless tribe whose sophisticated equipment - daggers, bows and arrows, and canoes - is beyond the comprehension of the simple Fa and Lok. At the same time, the new people, frightened by the strange-looking Neanderthals, are carrying on a placation ceremony. It is ironic that, although the new people are more intelligent than the Neanderthals, their religion is more debasing than that of the simpler tribe. The new people bow their heads before their antlered witch doctor. They have lost the simplicity of religion that the Neanderthals displayed in the burial of Mal. It is ironic, too, that the new people should practice such meaningless cruelty as the persecution of the Neanderthals. It is partly a result of their fear of the unknown. But, more than this, it is sport to kill these unusual-looking creatures. Because Golding reports the feelings, struggles, and tragedies of the Neanderthals immediately, causing us to identify with them, we view the human species, and perhaps ourselves, with chilling objectivity. We realize that the power of reason is no guarantee of human dignity. Parallels might be drawn between the behavior of the new people to the Neanderthals and exploitations by sophisticated modern man - perhaps the reader of the novel - of less educated and more vulnerable segments of society.

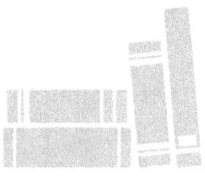

THE INHERITORS

TEXTUAL ANALYSIS

CHAPTER VII

....

Having returned to their own side of the river, Fa and Lok watch from hiding as the new people carry out a religious ceremony, placing on the ground clay and pelts in the shape of a stag, and then, after the appearance of a man dressed as a stag who performs a dance, stage a mutilation ritual in which one of the men, Tuami, chops off a finger of another, Pine-tree.

Comment

The hectic activities of the new people are a source of wonder to Lok and Fa, but to the reader they are evidence of a corrupt society. They walk upright and exhibit an ability to reason, but, terrified by the presence of the Neanderthals, they mutilate themselves in degrading religious rites, they decorate their skin with slivers of bone, and they fight among themselves.

Characters

Tuami: Calmly and efficiently, he cuts off the finger of a fellow tribesman. But in spite of his capacity for cruelty, he gives the impression of great strength and dignity. He is the second in command for the new people as Ha was for the Neanderthals.

Pine-tree, Chestnut-Head, Bush, Tuft: Warriors in the tribe of new people. Their names suggest that they are inhabitants of the forest rather than of the cave and, hence, more sophisticated than the Neanderthals.

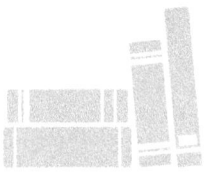

THE INHERITORS

TEXTUAL ANALYSIS

CHAPTER VIII

Fa and Lok see the new one in a canoe nursing at the breast of a fat woman. They see on the island Liku held on a leash by a young girl, Tanakil. Later, the new people are drinking from an animal skin full of strong spirits. After dark, the leader of the new people, Marlan, is discovered secretly eating a piece of meat. When the new people turn against him, he points to the hut where Liku is. She is killed and eaten, though Fa prevents Lok from seeing this.

Comment

Although the levels of society on the island are similar to those of the Neanderthals, with an old man in charge, aided by a strong wife and a physically superior second in command, and with several tribesmen of minor importance, cooperation and direction are lacking in the larger tribe. The observer beholds not the unity and fellowship of the Neanderthals but a turmoil of intrigue and violence presided over by Marlan who, in contrast to the strong and vigorous direction of Mal, encourages his people to indulge in drunken orgies so that he may be free to pursue his greedy schemes.

The cannibalism is meant to show that Homo sapiens exhibit all the bestial behavior credited to the Neanderthal man in the book's epigraph.

Characters

Marlan: A crafty old leader whose selfishness prompts the mutiny of his people. His nautical-sounding name suggests his mastery of travel by water.

Vivani: The fat woman who is married to Marlan.

Twal: A middle-aged woman with a crumpled face, the mother of Tanakil and probably Tuami's wife.

Tanakil: Twal's young daughter. Though she is Liku's mistress, she shows an affection for her.

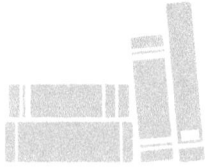

THE INHERITORS

TEXTUAL ANALYSIS

CHAPTER IX

At night, while most of the new people are drinking and Marlan is sleeping, his wife, Vivani, makes love to Tuami. When the camp is quiet, Lok and Fa steal in, only to be discovered and pursued. After eluding the new people, Lok discovers the trail of Fa, which leads to the edge of a swamp where he sees blood on the ground.

Comment

The return of Fa and Lok to the island camp of the new people is impractical and dangerous but they risk their lives because they want to recover the two children, Liku and the new one. Such natural affection as well as their mutual loyalty is a contrast to the wolfish self-indulgence of the new people. Lok and Fa look on in horror as Tuami and Vivani revel in a perverse love that finds expression in savage biting and clawing.

The character of Lok deepens in this chapter. On the one hand, the reader is made more aware of his animal qualities as he searches for Fa with eyes that see in the dark and with a nose that follows her scent. On the other, the humanity of Lok increases. His love for the children and for Fa become the center of his life. Also, after Fa organizes the raid on the new people and then is lost, Lok is forced to think for himself, and this new independence contributes to his manliness.

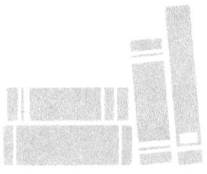

THE INHERITORS

TEXTUAL ANALYSIS

CHAPTER X

....

The new people, in the process of breaking camp, are rolling their canoes along a trail on logs. Lok watches them; then he sees Fa emerge from hiding in a swamp. Together they go to the empty camp, eat meat that the new people left as a sacrifice, and drink from a stone flask until they are so drunk that they begin to **parody** the actions of the new people.

Comment

In this chapter, Lok continues to grow. Imitating Mal, he becomes able to think like a man, not merely with pictures, but with a sense of the meaning of the word "like." The new people, he realizes, are fierce, like wolves; sweet, like honey; wild, like alcoholic beverages; powerful, like the waterfall; and knowledgeable, like gods. The poetry of his expression suggests that these new people are to Lok a divine people. But we can recognize in his lyric similes a definition of man that would apply today to the complex animal who brings to his rule of the world a mixture of beauty and destructiveness.

But not all of the knowledge of Lok is an improvement. He has expanded his mind to the degree that he can make analogies, but he has also acquired knowledge of evil, especially of the violent impulses in himself freed under the influence of strong drink. He even suggests, at one point, that Fa cut off his finger so that he will be like the new people. Such a tendency to self-destruction seems to be the price of acquiring a knowledge of the world.

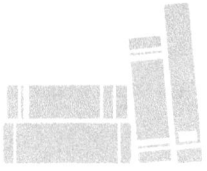

THE INHERITORS

TEXTUAL ANALYSIS

CHAPTER XI

A last attempt to recover the children, while the new people are preoccupied with the portage of their canoes past a waterfall, fails. Fa is chased onto a log floating on the river, which carries her to her death over the fall. Later in the day, Lok is alone, running on the cliff above the river. Finally he drops down to the earth.

Comment

The beastlike qualities of Fa and Lok are stressed at the end. Their device for recovering the children is one which birds and animals use: Fa is to distract the attention of the new people by showing herself on a mountain above them, while Lok is to slip in and steal the children. Lok, at the end, is described as red-skinned, hairy, and beastlike, with arms that hang to the ground. He "lopes" rather than runs, and his hand is now a "forepaw." The author refers to him as "it" rather than "he." And we see him sharply for the first time: "The head was set slightly forward on the strong neck that seemed to lead straight on to the row of curls under the lip. The mouth was wide and soft and above the curls of the upper lip the great nostrils were flared like wings. There was no bridge to the nose and the moonshadow of the jutting brow lay just above the tip." This use of the objective camera technique to depict the Neanderthal man in the way that Wells had described him is extremely ironic because the reader is aware of the inner life of the character of Lok, and shares in his human tragedy. As Lok recognizes the end of his people's existence, he emulates Mal, returning to the cave and lying down to die, in fetal position, amid the bones of his ancestors. With his death, the ice gods on the mountain fall amid tremendous noise, the representation of the cataclysmic change which heralds the age of man.

THE INHERITORS

TEXTUAL ANALYSIS

CHAPTER XII

A canoe is carrying the leaders of the new people along the river. They are glad to be free of the "forest devils" - the Neanderthals. Tanakil, who appears to be mad, is calling the name of Liku, who is dead. The new one is with his new mother, Vivani.

Comment

The use of an objective dramatic point of view at the end of Chapter XI has prepared us for a transition to the outlook of the new people in Chapter XII. Seeing the Neanderthals as devils, they have left behind in a cave an image of a Neanderthal, to ward off future attacks by evil spirits. Each tribe has interpreted the other as divine and malevolent. And the misunderstanding is greater on the part of the more highly developed society, the sophisticated and technologically superior Homo sapiens, who see the simple, kindly Neanderthals as diabolical creatures. Technology does not, apparently, ensure wisdom.

One man, Tuami, does achieve a self-realization that resembles the final maturing of Lok. He sees how evil the world is, and, with his conscience troubled by a sense of being "haunted, bedevilled, full of strange irrational grief," he is able to read the symbolic meaning of the journey. As the tribe of man moves from beneath to above the falls, he comes, not to the paradisiacal summer land sought by the Neanderthals, nor to the intellectual light that Tuami seeks, but to a further chaos. To the reader, the waterfall is perhaps an ironic reminder of the fall of man and of the residue of Original Sin which impedes the upward progress of every human being. Tuami's recognition of the universality of darkness causes him to give up his plan to kill Marlan with the spear he has been patiently sharpening. Such an action, he realizes, would do little to dispel the overall darkness.

The title, *The Inheritors*, is appropriate because it suggests the relationship that exists between the two tribes. The new people inherit the earth from the Neanderthals to make of it what they will. They have superior equipment. They have better minds. But intellect is no guarantee of the defeat of the predatory instinct. This applies not only to the early Homo sapiens inheriting characteristics from the Neanderthals, but to modern man, too, who often seems to be going forward only to be lost in the same chaos that threatens Tuami's group. Golding seems to be saying that increased technology is useless without an improvement of moral awareness. Further, the title provides an ironic comment on the realities of life. Christ promised in "The Sermon on the Mount" that the meek should inherit the earth. The opposite, however, seems to be the case as the meek Neanderthals are plowed under by their ruthless progeny. The meek, at the end of the novel, are as good as extinct, with only one member of the species, the new one, alive. Powerless to reproduce his kind, he has a value only as a symbol of the onus of guilt which man must bear for his previous barbarities.

In one sense this is a story of the first beginnings of the intellectual life. The cave which the Neanderthals inhabit is associated with Plato's cave of the universals. The natural wisdom of the Neanderthals which manifests itself in moments of mystical experience is an appreciation of the perfect forms remembered from previous existence. The Homo sapiens, lost on his island, is alienated from such wisdom, and so blunders frequently in his quest for a meaningful destiny.

From another viewpoint, this might be a story of a future age. Assume that the forest fire that destroyed most of the Neanderthals was an atomic war and that the present inhabitants of the world are humans retarded by the effects of radiation poisoning. Here is the beginning of another world whose members are wandering bands of primitive creatures learning all over again the rudimentary laws of survival so that sometime, aeons from now, they may once again achieve enough sophistication in weapons to obliterate themselves.

THE INHERITORS

CHARACTER ANALYSES

Lok

A developing character, at first he is silly and irresponsible, but later matures into a leader. In the final chapters of the novel he reveals a capacity for drawing comparisons, which is an indication that his mind is evolving toward human intelligence, and he learns to bear himself with a dignity that is appropriate to his tragic role.

Mal

The aged leader of the Neanderthals. Although he leads them too early to their summer camping area, he is generally wise and crafty and provident for the welfare of the tribe. His memory serves as a repository for the history of his people.

Ha

Vigorous and heroic, he takes over the leadership of the tribe when Mal becomes ill.

The Old Woman

The wife of Mal, wise and dignified, she tends the sick and provides leadership in the absence of Mal and Ha.

Fa

Lok's mate. Although she is stoical and brave, she senses the responsibility that she bears to her progeny and so she is more inclined to be cautious than is Lok.

Nil

A nursing mother who is probably Ha's mate.

Liku

A young girl, a playmate of Lok's, possibly his sister. She is kidnapped by the new people.

The New One

Nil's baby boy who represents the future of the Neanderthals. At the end of the novel he is carried off by the new people, the one surviving member of the tribe.

Marlan

The old man who leads the tribe of Homo sapiens. He is cruel and selfishly clever, ruling by fear and trickery and by the exploitation of the superstitious beliefs of his people.

Tuami

Marlan's second in command who steals his wife. But though he is vicious and deceitful, there is an attractive calmness to Tuami. He is the only character to achieve a recognition of his own guilt.

Pine-Tree, Chestnut-Head, Bush, Tuft

Names given by Lok to some of Marlan's warriors.

Vivani

The fat and luxuriant wife of Marlan and mistress of Tuami. She pampers herself with splendid furs. Having recently lost a baby of her own, she is able to nurse the new one.

Twal

A middle-aged woman with a crumpled face, the mother of Tanakil and probably the mate of Tuami.

Tanakil

A young girl, a playmate of Liku after Liku is captured. She is only beginning to learn to be as cruel as the other new people.

PINCHER MARTIN

TEXTUAL ANALYSIS

CHAPTERS 1 AND 2

Christopher Martin, lone survivor of a torpedoed British warship, is floating on a life belt in the Atlantic. Coming to the edge of an island rock, he struggles forward, ingeniously using limpets as hand and footholds to scale the rock.

Comment

The journey of Christopher Martin is symbolic, representing a process of self-discovery. There are two poles in Christopher's personality. He is Pincher Martin, grasping, selfish, conniving, as determined to satisfy his instincts as a lobster. He is Christopher-Christ bearer-making a difficult trip across water, in the manner of Saint Christopher, as a test of his spiritual potential. As the story develops, he fails to realize this potential, and so is destroyed.

Christopher, as we see him, is literally without direction, subject to the motions of waves and currents. We later learn that these are appropriate circumstances, for his life has been a meaningless submission to pressures of pleasure and pain. His present situation is representative of his career as citizen and sailor. The first quality that reveals itself as he struggles up the rocky slope of the island is his instinct for preservation. He is, as he remarks, "Like a limpet." (A limpet is a large mollusk with a conical shell and a broad flat base that grips rocks or timber by suction). Tough, elastic, hard-shelled, adapted to the struggle with sea and rock, the limpets are representations of Christopher, the mere instinctual being. Later, as the personality of Christopher expands and we know of his greedy, selfish past, the symbol of the lobster, made more formidable by his claws, becomes appropriate to the character.

By his rendering of concrete detail as seen by Christopher, Golding makes us share the struggle for survival. We feel his weightlessness in the water. We feel the pebbles against his cheek as he struggles up the rocky shore. After establishing this empathy, or sense of identity, between reader and character, Golding can go on to give us the sordid details of Christopher's life without risking the loss of our sympathy.

It should be mentioned that most of the novel is hallucinatory. In Chapter 1, as he floats in the water, Christopher thinks he is kicking off his heavy seaboots. At the end of the novel we learn that he died wearing his seaboots, and we are forced to conclude that the entire struggle for survival is imaginary, the projection of a mind obsessed with the idea of self-preservation.

PINCHER MARTIN

TEXTUAL ANALYSIS

CHAPTERS 3 AND 4

Coming to in a trench he is tempted to despair, but drives himself forward. He is determined to pit what he has, his slicker, life belt, and knife against the elements. His first thought is for shelter. He discovers, under a slab of stone leaning against a side of the trench, an opening large enough for him to crawl into. Thinking back, he recalls his friend Nat sitting precariously on the rail of the ship, his face in his hands. He crawls from the trench to search for fresh water. Eventually he discovers a small cave containing a pool left by the rain. Encouraged, he drags rocks to the highest part of the island to stand as a rescue signal. He builds a three-foot high pyramid of four boulders resembling a dwarf. Thinking of food, he forces himself to eat sea anemones, soft, red, flower-like animals clinging to the rock.

Comment

Most of the struggles of Christopher are on the level of survival. He goes through primitive stages of social development, like those of the boys on the island in *Lord of the Flies*, and the savage creatures in *The Inheritors*. He instinctively works for shelter, water, and food, just as any beast does. But then, since he is a man, his struggle goes beyond mere survival as he thinks about rescue, and builds a replica of a man out of stone. This stone dwarf is symbolic. Christopher's whole existence on the island will be devoted to building an image of a man-himself-in his own mind. Christopher does not yet realize how perfectly the stone dwarf mirrors himself. As in the Castle Rock **episodes** of *Lord of the Flies*, the stone represents the hardness of heart of the persons connected with it. This is the material he has to work with-rock-in creating a human personality. His efforts are limited by circumstances of setting and also, symbolically, by the spiritual deprivations in his own soul. The stone beckons to passing ships by saying, "Here I am; I am a man." But it also reveals that this man is a man of stone, a man without human feeling. So far, then, the definition of man is limited. Christopher shows the instincts of the animal-the anemone or the limpet. And he shows the intelligence to make patterns out of stone. One other manifestation of human awareness is present in Christopher's friend Nat, meditating as he sits on the ship's rail. Like Simon, in *Lord of the Flies*, Nat is a religious man. But so far, this part of Christopher is unawakened.

Character Analyses

Christopher - intelligent, selfish, aggressive, a man with an enormous need to survive in the flesh because he possesses no knowledge of the spirit.

Nathaniel - a foil to Christopher. A religious mystic.

PINCHER MARTIN

TEXTUAL ANALYSIS

CHAPTERS 5 AND 6

....

He recalls that Nat had predicted his death and had warned him that, because of the condition of his soul, his afterlife would be a complete negation, with a "black lightning destroying everything that we call life." He had called Nat a fool, and denied that he was soon to die. Now he continues that denial by hanging onto life on the rock. He cracks the shells of mussels and eats the bodies to keep his flesh alive. He goes through the identification pictures and papers in his pocket so as to preserve his identity. He builds his rock statue to four feet by placing a large stone at the base. He controls his existence by imposing names on his immediate surroundings, for example, Gull Cliff, Food Cliff, High Street, and Picadilly. When he begins to name the nearby island rocks, "the Teeth," he is horrified at the thought that he is living inside these "Teeth."

Comment

Nat, like Simon, makes an accurate prophecy that is not believed. Later, when we learn that all of Christopher's experiences on the island are imaginary, we realize how much his hell is a complete negation of life. Not only is he deprived of all of the human pleasures that he is used to, but the whole experience becomes nothing but a figment of the imagination of a drowning man who refuses to believe in his inevitable death. When Christopher confidently asserts that his life on the island is "the ordinary experience of living," he is revealing that the ordinary experience of living is, too, an illusion. All of his life is just a barren existence as that on the rock, a chain of selfish gestures, of seductions and betrayals.

Two important and related symbols are established in these chapters-teeth and Chinese boxes. Christopher, who has always eaten the weaker person, devouring them with his hands, or his mouth, or his body, is now being devoured-as if he is a mouth inside another mouth, which is inside other mouths. The sets of teeth are arranged inside each other like Chinese boxes. That is what makes the teeth-like rocks so frightening. They are devouring his life and sanity just as he has done to others, and he is terrified at the fittingness of the retribution. He realizes that his is no longer the largest mouth in a world rapacious mouths. Just as the mussels are his food, so he is food to the larger forces of destruction represented in the looming rocks. The thought of these enormous teeth around him is so horrifying that, at the end of Chapter 6, he cannot sleep.

PINCHER MARTIN

TEXTUAL ANALYSIS

CHAPTERS 7 AND 8

Martin thinks of the past. He recalls an interview with his commanding officer before he received his commission. He thinks of when he was a civilian, an actor, and of his affair with his producer's wife. Returning to the present, he takes a silver candy wrapper from his pocket and ties it on the head of the stone dwarf, so that it shines in the sun. Then, as a signal to passing airplanes, he heaps up seaweed in the pattern of a cross. While he is gathering seaweed close to the shore, the sight of a lobster sends him scurrying onto the rock shuddering with loathing. His agitated mind ranges so freely that he forgets the immediate task and thinks back to when he was ordered by his producer to take, as a second part, one of the seven deadly sins-Greed, because he was born with "both hands out to grab." As his thoughts flit about, he begins to fear that he is going mad.

Comment

Although the point of view becomes omniscient author at the end, throughout most of the novel Golding stays in the mind of the central character. As he follows his thoughts, at times he uses the stream of consciousness technique to follow the chain of associations in Christopher's mind. As he thinks of life on the ship and of the commander asking him about his profession, he is reminded of his conversation with the producer's wife. Rather than follow a logical order, Golding recreates the thoughts of his **protagonist** as they are tied together in memory.

It is appropriate that Chris should be an actor. He has played many parts before, and now he is acting a life that does not exist. Though dead, he is forced to go through the pretense of living- even to building a seaweed cross to mark his place of death, his Golgotha. His cross represents intellectual ingenuity alone, not spiritual or moral insight. The reason he loathes the lobster is that it suggests this lack. The lobster and he are on the same level of existence. With "both hands out to grab," he is like a clawing primordial creature with greed his overriding drive.

Character Analyses

Peter - a weak character, a drunkard. Christopher's producer.

Helen - Peter's wife, cheap in language and manner. Christopher's mistress.

George - the director who works with Christopher and Peter.

PINCHER MARTIN

TEXTUAL ANALYSIS

CHAPTERS 9 AND 10

As if trying to recover his identity, Christopher is searching in the pool for his reflection. Feverish from food poisoning, his delirium increases and he hears again a drunken speech by Pete, his director, comparing him to a maggot eating other maggots. A lick of summer lightning reminds him of a similar flash shining across the face of Mary (later the wife of Nat) as he attempted to seduce her in his car. He recalls, as a boy, smashing the bicycle of Peter because it was better than his. He thinks back to his attempts to escape the draft, and how his producer, Peter, and director, George, refused to support his deferment. Even Helen, his mistress, refused to help him because she had found out about his other women.

Comment

The things that caught up with Christopher in civilian life are catching up now. That he cannot see his reflection in the water is possibly related to the folk tradition in which a ghost, or vampire, or similar deathly apparition leaves no reflection in a mirror. The lobsters that crawl nearby are mirror enough for him. They suggest that he is a creature who grabs, without consciousness of wrongdoing, whatever morsels come within his reach. As his thoughts run again and again to the same scenes-his betrayal of others and their betrayal of him-he begins to see himself as a creature of prey like an enormous maggot who has fed on all of the other maggots locked in a tin box. Pete had given him a description of this process of preparing a Chinese delicacy. The maggots within maggots are, of course, like the other images of teeth within teeth, Chinese boxes, receding mirrors, and large and small shellfish. At the end of Chapter 10, Christopher unconsciously identifies himself with the superior maggot who eats all of the others when he asserts, "I'll live if I have to eat everything else on this bloody box!"

Character Analysis

Mary-beautiful and strong-willed, elegant but tough.

PINCHER MARTIN

TEXTUAL ANALYSIS

CHAPTERS 11 AND 12

....

A terrible despair is seizing the lone man as he thinks of his illness and solitude. A gull that flashes by is, to his distraught eyes, a "flying lizard." Eventually, he gets the poison out of his system by filling his lifebelt with water and using it as an enema. But his feeling of triumph gives way to further hallucination as he see a red lobster swimming in the sea. He awakens from a fit to find his pants torn and bloody and his head bruised. Rain comes, and then lightning that shears off a slice of rock and leaves a black scar, reminding him of the "black lightning" predicted by Nat.

Comment

At the end of Chapter 12, Christopher is trying to convince himself that he is mad. He would prefer insanity to the awful realization that this rock is his appropriate hell, the logical outcome of the crimes he has committed. Even when he tries to avoid blame, however, he makes **allusions** to his guilt. For example, when he refers to the gull as a "lizard," and when he blames his despair on his poisoned colon, "the serpent... coiled in my own body," he is calling up a traditional image of evil, the serpent, Satan, existing in Christopher as he did in the boys in *Lord of the Flies*. Further, since the serpent is a conventional symbol for the id, the source of man's primitive urges, according to Freud, especially the sexual urge, it is a fitting reminder of his dissolute past. Christopher Martin's id has run berserk. And now he must pay for his previous failure to coordinate activities of mind and body, by the complete loss of association between mind and body. Madness is preferable to the cool light of reason. Madness, he realizes, is an escape from responsibility and the black lighting. So, an actor to the end, he mimics the mad scenes from Shakespeare's *King Lear*.

PINCHER MARTIN

TEXTUAL ANALYSIS

CHAPTERS 13 AND 14

The storm continues, and Chris, in his raving, persists in trying to shout it down. The Dwarf is blown over and he imagines he sees in its place an old woman, and then the old woman becomes God, asking him if he has had enough. He shouts that he prefers the torture of endurance to submission to the black lightning. Finally, as he rants and raves, lightning strikes the rock, completing the destruction of the protagonist.

In the final chapter, a British officer lands on an island in the Hebrides to claim a body, which turns out to be that of Christopher Martin. The body has been thrown up on shore. When the Scotsman who inhabits the island asks the officer whether there is any surviving for someone like Christopher, the officer takes him to be asking about the suffering of the victim, and he assures him that there was not much surviving. "You saw the body. He didn't even have time to kick off his seaboots."

Comment

While Chris is having his shouting battle with God, he claims to have created this God, and also to be able to create his own heaven. "You have created it," answers God, implying that the island rock is a heaven (or hell) of Christopher's own making. We learn conclusively that the island is a representation of an afterlife with the announcement that Chris did not remove his seaboots. The entire experience on the island has been a dream of a drowning man, an extension of his human life beyond the actual, as a punishment for his graspingness, in the same way that the characters in Dante's Inferno are punished by being forced to recreate, symbolically, their human sins in their own private chamber of hell.

What Mr. Campbell, the islander, wants from Officer Davidson is some word from an expert on the possibility of an afterlife. The answer is doubly false, because Chris has not only endured, he has endured beyond the present life into an eternity of damnation. The whole experience of Christopher in the novel reasserts the actuality of hell. Golding has written one **episode** more to be tacked on the end of Dante's Inferno.

It is appropriate that the lightning which terminates Christopher's experiences on the rock is compared to a claw of a lobster. He has made his hell and his God out of his own lobsterlike instincts, and those instincts ultimately exterminate him. The penalty for a man who lives for himself without using reason to control his vicious tendencies, and without using reason to orient himself to his fellow man, is complete obliteration.

PINCHER MARTIN

CHARACTER ANALYSES

Christopher Martin

A man of great tenacity but little morality. His philosophy of life is eat or be eaten. He uses his good looks and ingenuity to further his own selfish egotistical aims. The only affection he has ever felt is for his friend Nat. Nevertheless, at one point, he contemplates killing Nat out of jealousy. His civilian profession is acting.

Nathaniel Walterson

A religious prophet not unlike Simon in *Lord of the Flies*. He is a friend of Christopher's solicitous for his spiritual well-being, generous and warmhearted. He marries Mary, the one girl who withstands the seductive charm of Christopher.

Mary

Beautiful and strong-willed, she chooses Nat over Christopher. She is a complex person, with elegance and refinement combined with toughness of speech and moral fibre.

Helen

Fat and white and crude, the producer's wife who Christopher seduces.

Peter

A childhood friend and later his producer. Frequently, when he is drunk, he makes vicious verbal attacks on Christopher.

George

A director of plays.

Mr. Davidson

A captain in the English Navy who is responsible for recovering the body of Christopher.

Mr. Campbell

The Scottish islander who first finds Christopher's body.

FREE FALL

TEXTUAL ANALYSIS

CHAPTER I

....

Sammy Mountjoy, a bastard born of a drunken mother in a rural slum, is recalling his life. His first expansion of human relationships beyond his mother and the boarder upstairs occurs when he goes to public school and meets Evie, a habitual liar who tells tales of her fabulous relatives.

Comment

We later learn that Sammy Mountjoy is an artist who, serving as a soldier in World War II, is captured by the Germans. The crucial experience in the narrative is an interrogation in which he undergoes a form of psychological torture, which forces him to a realization of the poverty of his moral resources. Retracing his childhood experiences, he hopes to answer two questions: when did he become the person he is now? and when did he lose freedom of choice? The narrative focuses on Sammy's development as an artist and as a man. For example, the ease with which his mother and Evie exploit his ready faith illustrates his sensitivity of imagination and also his lack of strength of character.

The point of view that Golding uses in this novel is an outgrowth of previous experiments. The omniscient author point of view became more concentrated in each of his two previous novels. Where in *Lord of the Flies* he ranged freely from character to character, in *The Inheritors* he limited the outlook in the central chapters to the character Lok. In *Pincher Martin* he stayed within the mind of Christopher until the last chapter. And finally this tendency to stay within the consciousness of the main character leads him in *Free Fall* to adopt the technique of the first person narrative, allowing Sammy, as protagonist, to tell his own story.

Characters

Sammy Mountjoy: Born out of wedlock in a slum neighborhood, he triumphs over his environment and becomes an artist. For a poor boy, and one who is constantly in trouble, the name Mountjoy might seem ironic, but actually his childhood is, in spite of hardship, a time of relative freedom and joy because he is still innocent.

Mrs. Mountjoy: An immoral and boisterous woman but a good mother.

Evie: A congenital liar, about six years old, who stimulates the imagination of Sammy.

FREE FALL

TEXTUAL ANALYSIS

CHAPTER II

....

Sammy recalls the two boyhood friends who influenced him. Johnny Spragg, rough and independent, leads Sammy on two dangerous nighttime excursions, one to an airport and another to the estate of a general. Philip Arnold, a more sinister personality, on one occasion persuades Sammy to mistreat the younger boys at school, and on another dares him to defile a church by spitting on the altar. Sammy is invariably caught in the act, but Philip goes free.

Comment

The human encounters in this chapter show Sammy in his innocence moving through increasingly complex moral contexts without being changed. Johnny represents one type of commitment; he is the young adventurer, the hero of boyhood storybooks. But somehow his intrepid leadership seems poorly directed in a world of generals and airports and threatening darkness. Philip represents an opposing view of life. He manipulates other people and takes perverse pleasure in getting them into trouble. In inducing Sammy to defile the church, he comes to represent a diabolical force.

The incident in the church occasions a still more complex moral encounter. After he spits, Sammy is caught and struck by the church custodian who drags him before the parson, who represents the attitude of the adult world, insisting that Sammy tell why he performed the act because he is certain that such an act must be part of a plot against his church. The why of course does not exist. Sammy has not yet committed himself to sin, but has merely given in to the stronger personality of Philip.

Characters

Johnny Spragg: A boyhood chum of Sammy's whose love for airplanes and adventure is the stimulus for the dangerous expeditions on which he leads his friend.

Philip Arnold: Even in childhood his warped personality compels him to destroy the ideals of himself and others. He enjoys manipulating others and he relishes their pain.

Father Watts-Watt: A kindly parson, shy and withdrawing and apparently homosexual. He shows signs of a persecution complex in conjuring up a conspiracy against himself.

The Verger: The church custodian who strikes Sammy and then is repentant.

Father Anselm: Fr. Watts-Watt's young curate.

FREE FALL

TEXTUAL ANALYSIS

CHAPTER III

At the end of Chapter II, Sammy was in the hospital being treated for an ear infection which had apparently been aggravated when the verger struck him. In Chapter III Sammy is recovering in the hospital, where he hears of his mother's death. He is visited by the verger and by Father Watts-Watt, who adopts him as his ward.

Comment

From the impressions recorded in this chapter it becomes clear that the distinctive element in Sammy's character is not any commitment but rather his ability to withhold commitment. When his mother dies, he reacts briefly, but after a night's sleep is able to forget her. When the verger visits him, he is able neither to blame nor forgive because he recognizes the man's guiltlessness as well as his own. With Father Watts-Watt, who offers him compassion, he feels no desire to communicate.

But although his attitude towards life is becoming increasingly cynical, he has still not become the person he is to be. He has not fallen.

FREE FALL

TEXTUAL ANALYSIS

CHAPTER IV

Chapter IV skips ahead approximately eight years. Sammy, nineteen, is an art student in love with a girl named Beatrice. Their courtship begins when he arranges a "chance" meeting outside of her college. He is also, at this time, interested in political revolution. He brings his boyhood friend, Philip, to a Communist Party meeting.

Comment

In spite of an increasingly cynical outlook, Sammy is still an idealist. This is reflected in his political faith in Communism and in his adoration of a beautiful girl. His Beatrice resembles the Beatrice whom Dante praised in sonnets and in *The Divine Comedy*. She possesses an ideal beauty and, for a time at least, chastity.

But in Sammy's commitments there are present the seeds of disintegration. As Philip points out, the Communist meeting is absurd since, except for one worker, it consists solely of professional people: parsons, librarians, and teachers. With Beatrice a disillusionment is inevitable since, in contrast to her glowing fleshly beauty, her spirit is a limp rag. Her attitudes are domestic and conservative. She is a girl who can occasionally say maybe, but never yes.

Beautiful and seemingly inaccessible, Beatrice Ifor is the girl of Sammy's dreams. We later learn that she attended the same secondary school as Sammy. At present she is studying to be a school teacher.

FREE FALL

TEXTUAL ANALYSIS

CHAPTER V

....

When Sammy seduces Beatrice, he destroys the ideal that she represents. Not only is she now accessible, but she hardly seems worth the trouble because she is sexually frigid. And her conversation, limited to a few stock responses, is extremely boring.

Comment

After seducing Beatrice, Sammy asks her, "Don't you feel anything?" Her answer is characteristic: "I don't know. Maybe." As if to evoke from her passive nature a definite response, Sammy begins to indulge in cruelties in his lovemaking and in his use of her as an artist's model. He forces her to recognize her own flesh and he destroys for her, as for himself, the possibility of the life of the spirit. As Sammy emulates the manner of Philip and develops a posture of sadism, his unhappiness increases. He is filled with contempt for the flesh and for the brutish activities of sensual man, but he is incapable of believing in the possibility of any better life for himself as an individual.

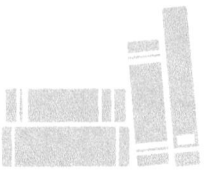

FREE FALL

TEXTUAL ANALYSIS

CHAPTER VI

Eventually Sammy leaves Beatrice for a girl named Taffy, whom he meets at a Communist rally. Ignoring the distraught pleas of Beatrice, who writes to him and goes to his friends asking for his address, he marries Taffy. In a short while he leaves the Communist Party out of a feeling of indifference.

Comment

This brings Sammy to the point where he enters the service as a war artist. He still has not discovered his present self in past history, nor does he accept his guilt; but he begins to understand his loss of free will. He sees that it was manifest in his relations with Beatrice when he began to treat her with vicious disregard. To do so was to give away his freedom and to become something less than human.

At this point Sammy has become a moral anarchist. He welcomes the war because "There was anarchy in the mind where I lived and anarchy in the world at large, two states so similar that one might have produced the other." And, indeed one did produce the other. The diseased mind produced the diseased world. Sammy's failure to comprehend his guilt in the late 1930's is symptomatic of the general failure of mankind. He is an ironic figure - intelligent, but blind to his sin of negligence, too callous to interpret his own moral position. His real crime, like that of Christopher Martin, is a lack of self-knowledge. He represents the failure of the liberal intellectual, through indifference, to provide a bulwark against human cruelty.

Taffy: Sammy's wife, is amoral and strong-willed and has a more outgoing personality than has Beatrice. In her rugged hardihood and political activism she represents a foil to the shy Beatrice.

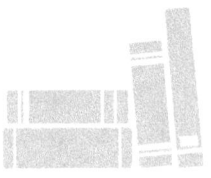

FREE FALL

TEXTUAL ANALYSIS

CHAPTER VII

Sammy, a prisoner of war, is brought before a psychologist, Dr. Halde, a civilian member of the Gestapo. Halde wants information about escape plans. When Sammy insists that he knows nothing about such plans, he is taken out and blindfolded.

Comment

Sammy's position has been again reversed. As Philip worked upon him, and as he worked upon Beatrice, so now Dr. Halde, the professional sadist, takes over. A university professor turned inquisitor, Halde suggests the disturbed condition of the world in which torturing has become a general way of life.

In his relationship with Halde, as in many of his human encounters, Sammy goes through a process of disillusionment. When he first meets Halde, he thinks that he could like him because he seems so civilized. But then the mask crumbles and Halde becomes the ruthless torturer. Yet, in Halde's characterization of his victim as a man of no strong commitments to ideas or nation, and an easy subject for torture, Sammy is prodded to a modicum of self-realization.

Like Philip, Dr. Halde enjoys watching the agony of others. He is a university psychologist who has adapted his professional skills to the service of the Gestapo.

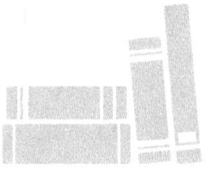

FREE FALL

TEXTUAL ANALYSIS

CHAPTER VIII

....

As he recalls the blindfold, Sammy is reminded of the first night of his adoption by Fr. Watts-Watt, when the darkness in his room in the parsonage filled him with terror. Fr. Watts-Watt comes into the room and makes advances. Then he begins to cry out against his imaginary enemies.

Comment

Like Halde, Father Watts-Watt is an occasion of disillusionment as his homosexualism and paranoia become apparent to the boy. It is as if both of these men are substitute fathers for the fatherless Sammy, being tested in positions of authority, but failing to provide a reliable authority.

Although the quest and character of Sammy Mountjoy are more complex than those of the characters in earlier fables, the characters whom he encounters are part of a representative pattern. Just as Philip and Johnny represent diverse male friendships to Sammy, so Beatrice and Taffy, opposite types of womanhood, represent contrary possibilities of fulfillment, and Father Watts-Watt and Dr. Halde are poles apart as figures of adult authority. It might be possible to say that Golding is suggesting the value of the via media, except that it would be impossible to strike a middle way between these pairs of perverted personalities without falling into a distorted position. Halfway between Fr. Watts-Watt and Halde is an adult Philip. Rather, it would seem that Golding is simplifying the world in order to suggest the magnitude of Sammy's experience. In his encounters with Fr. Watts-Watt and Halde, Sammy is being educated to the nature of a blind, destructive perversity which is as universal as man.

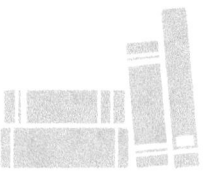

FREE FALL

TEXTUAL ANALYSIS

CHAPTER IX

....

When he removes his blindfold, he is still shrouded in darkness. Feeling along the wall, he realizes that he is in a small cell. His imagination tells him that some terrible object is in the center of the cell. He touches a slimy lump of dead matter which reminds him of human flesh and he imagines a corpse hanging from the ceiling.

Comment

Knowing that he is dealing with the sensitive personality of an artist, Halde devises a psychological torture to work upon the imagination of Sammy. He places him in frightening darkness and then brings him in contact with what seems to be a segment of a corpse. He lets Sammy's artistic faculty do the rest. Though there is no body hanging from the ceiling, the suggestion of that possibility is worse than actuality. This implies that the evil in Sammy's world is actually in himself and of his own making. At the end of the chapter, as he cries for help, he is recognizing, however confusedly, the inadequacy of himself. He is seeing, too, his own nature as resembling a piece of dead flesh.

FREE FALL

TEXTUAL ANALYSIS

CHAPTER X

....

When the commandant lets Sammy out of his cell, it is as if he has died and entered a new world. The setting around him has become harmonious in form. But the world within him is still ugly and loathsome.

Comment

Sammy, although existing in a condition of mental shock, makes two important discoveries in this chapter. The first is that the world has lost the "substance" which was the basis for its order. "The brilliance of our political vision and the profundity of our scientific knowledge had enabled us to dispense with this substance." This is the same indictment against progress uttered in *The Inheritors*. The world has sacrificed love for technology: "This substance was a kind of vital morality, not the relationship of a man to remote posterity nor even to a social system, but the relationship of individual man to individual man - once an irrelevance but now seen to be the forge in which all change, all value, all life is beaten out into a good or bad shape." The second discovery concerns himself as, looking within, he sees a frightening and loathsome reality. His betrayal of Beatrice he views as an inevitable result in a chain of evil actions over which he had no control because he himself was already an evil person. His reminiscences turn toward the period between innocence and evil, the years of his secondary schooling. It is here that he hopes to pinpoint the moment in which he lost freedom.

FREE FALL

TEXTUAL ANALYSIS

CHAPTER XI

....

Recalling his years of secondary school, Sammy's impressions center on Nick Shales, a science teacher and freethinker, and Rowena Pringle, a teacher of religion. The kindness of the atheist, Nick, contrasts with the cruelty of Miss Pringle, who is carrying a torch for Father Watts-Watt.

Comment

Golding again uses a dialectic to present the issues in Sammy's mental development. Miss Pringle is put on one side of him and Nick Shales on the other. They might be compared to good and bad angels hovering over an individual in a religious painting, except that it would be impossible to say which of the two teachers is the good angel. Both are completely committed to their views of the world: Miss Pringle sees the universe as being directed by an Old Testament God of power and frightful retribution, and Nick sees the universe as an exact system which submits to rational analysis. At this time Sammy chooses the position of Nick because of the cruel sarcasm of Miss Pringle. But later he will realize that each system is in itself inadequate to explain a dualistic universe.

Religion, hatred, and frustrated sexuality give to Rowena Pringle's personality a distorted cast. She reads an obscene meaning into a sketch of Sammy's done in her class.

A kindly atheist, Nick Shales, is one of several temporary "fathers" of Sammy. He supports a scientific view of the universe with a poetic vision.

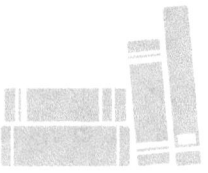

FREE FALL

TEXTUAL ANALYSIS

CHAPTER XII

....

Two events occur which increase Sammy's cynicism. He gives a sketch of Beatrice's to Philip to pass as his own, and the art teacher praises the drawing. A scandal occurs at the school when it is learned that the French teacher and the rugby coach are having an affair.

Comment

This is the time in Sammy's life when he, becomes his adult self. It is the time when he loses religious and moral sensitivity, and when he loses a sense of contact with others. On Nick Shale's scientific liberalism, he builds a completely selfish philosophy of life. And when the possession of Beatrice Ifor becomes his major interest, he expresses his willingness to sacrifice everything else for her. The headmaster of his school emerges as another substitute father in this chapter as he encourages Sammy, who is graduating, to pursue his art with complete commitment. But Sammy instead devotes himself to the acquisition and "utter abjection" of Beatrice. This is the point at which sin takes over as the strongest element in Sammy's personality. The effect is not traceable to any one act but is a result of a failure of humanity and of vision; Sammy has lost contact with his fellow man.

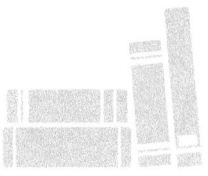

FREE FALL

TEXTUAL ANALYSIS

CHAPTER XIII

After the war, Sammy visits Beatrice in a sanitarium where she has been confined for seven years. Her only response to his presence is to urinate on the floor. The doctor in charge, who is in love with Sammy's wife, berates him: "You use everyone. You used that woman. You used Taffy. And now you've used me." Sammy admits, "Yes. It's all my fault."

Comment

The worlds of childhood and adulthood merge in these last chapters. The general's home, which Sammy once explored in the dead of night with Johnny Spragg, has been converted into the insane asylum where Beatrice is confined. Beatrice, when she urinates in his presence, recalls an imbecile girl, Minnie, who in the infant school urinated on the shoes of a visitor. For Sammy, the past and present, near and far, authority and revolt, flesh and spirit come together because he realizes that both worlds, that of science and that of morality, that of the objective and that of the subjective, do exist in him. There is a chain of cause and effect in the lives of those around him and of himself. Beatrice is in the asylum probably because of the frustration of her love for him. He cut off this love because of who he is, and he is who he is because of the forces working on him, the examples and influences which make themselves felt. Perhaps from one point of view Beatrice is being punished for her sins, but from another, he is responsible for her sins and his own, and is accordingly punished by a torture of the mind. He realizes finally that he must recognize his crimes in order to be a whole person. He must recognize the dark side of the human spirit.

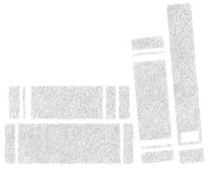

FREE FALL

TEXTUAL ANALYSIS

CHAPTER XIV

....

Sammy goes to the hospital to visit Nick Shales, intending to refute his atheism, but withdraws in silence, awed by the dignity of the dying man. He goes to Miss Pringle to ease her guilt at mistreating him. But, before he can speak, she reveals her complete lack of a sense of guilt; she praises his art and hopes that she has been, in some way, responsible for his success. His recollections shift to his removal from the prison cell and the commandant's strange apology: "The Herr Doctor does not know about peoples."

Comment

When the commandant says that Halde does not know "peoples," he is grammatically incorrect but thematically exact. Halde can define the individual with great accuracy, as he does with Sammy. But he leaves out of his consideration the most important part of man, the spirit. "For this mode which we must call the spirit breathes through the universe and does not touch it; touches only the dark things, held prisoner, incommunicado, touches, judges, sentences and passes on." Sammy realizes that in his prison experience, his physical eyes closed and his flesh and imagination tormented, he came in touch with the spirit. When Halde tries to deal with the soul of man with scientific methods, he leaves out the darkness and shadows of spirit, and accordingly, misinterprets his victim.

Sammy reflected in Chapter II, "Man is not an instantaneous creature, nothing but a physical body and the reaction of the moment. He is an incredible bundle of miscellaneous memories and feelings, of fossils and coral growths." If this is true, then a part of the bundle is the impulse toward anarchy and the need for recognition of this impulse - a need present not only in Sammy but in those characters who prey upon others, including Halde, Miss Pringle, and Philip. And it is equally present in characters of innocence such as Johnny Spragg, Nick Shales, and Beatrice. As Sammy observes on the last page of the novel, the disparate worlds of Nick Shales and Rowena Pringle are both real and their integrity is inviolable. But "There is no bridge." Perhaps it is Sammy's responsibility as an artist and man to provide a link between alien demands of spirit and mind.

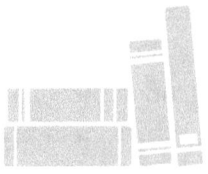

FREE FALL

CHARACTER ANALYSES

Sammy Mountjoy

All his life an outsider because he was born out of wedlock in a slum neighborhood. A talented artist who at first believes he is above conventional morality, he spends his life searching for something, perhaps a father, perhaps a code, to give his existence meaning. Ultimately, he discovers his own identity and his own guilt, and this makes all previous knowledge obsolete.

Beatrice Ifor

When Sammy first pursues her, she is beautiful and inaccessible, the ideal girl of his dreams. When he seduces her, she becomes listless and subdued. Finally, after he deserts her, she becomes a hopeless case in a mental institution. Because of her lack of imagination and her strict conventionalism, she is a foil to the artist Sammy, who makes his own morality.

Johnny Spragg

Generous and goodhearted and somewhat a hero to Sammy because of his adventurousness. Sammy's last sight of him is on a motorcycle with a girl, kissing on a blind hill-top. He dies in the war as a flyer.

Philip Arnold

Devious, self-protective, and cynical. He not only enjoys getting other people into trouble, but delights in destroying their ideals. At the end, he is an important official in the British government.

Taffy

Simple, healthy, and amoral, she speaks with rough, masculine force. Her character is much more definite than Beatrice's and this makes her a match for Sammy, whom she marries. Responding naturally and without inhibition, she easily manages the transition from active Communist to homemaker and mother.

Evie

A childhood companion and influence on Sammy's imagination. A congenital liar, her marvelous tales lift Sammy out of the narrow dimensions of his home in Rotten Row.

Mrs. Mountjoy

In spite of poverty, and in spite of her drinking and promiscuity, she brings to her son Sammy a love and willingness to tell romantic tales that stimulate his affections and imagination. She is a shrew to her neighbors but a perfect mother to Sammy, and she is one of the few characters in the book who do not deliberately hurt other people.

Dr. Halde

A kindly atheist, one of several substitute wartime role as torturer. In attempting to elicit a confession from Sammy, he goads his victim to self-recognition. He is, like Philip, a person who gives in to his destructive impulses and makes of cruelty a pleasant profession.

Rowena Pringle

A teacher of religion who is, like Halde, vicious. She thinks nothing of preaching God and hatred at the same time. Her love for Sammy's guardian, Fr. Watts-Watt, makes her all the more cruel and repressive in her treatment of Sammy. It is her violent animosity toward him that drives Sammy away from Christianity.

Nick Shales

A kindly atheist, one of several substitute fathers of Sammy. A science teacher who believes in the rationality of the physical world, he provides a contrast to Miss Pringle during Sammy's secondary school years.

Father Watts-Watt

Another familiar substitute, but one who reveals homosexual feelings towards Sammy. He is a generous man who adopts Sammy after his mother's death, but he is guilt-ridden and paranoid in his fear of imaginary enemies.

The Verger

Remorseful after striking Sammy on the head, an uncertain warrior in the camp of Father Watts-Watt.

Father Anselm

It is because of Philip's attraction to Father Anselm, Father Watts-Watt's curate, which embarrasses Philip, that he prompts Sammy to desecrate the church.

Kenneth Endicott

The psychiatrist in charge of the asylum where Beatrice is confined. He expresses anger towards Sammy because he is in love with his wife, Taffy, and blames Sammy for destroying the happiness of all who come in contact with him. But, like Haled, he is an example of the doctor who cannot heal himself.

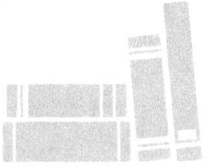

FREE FALL

ESSAY QUESTIONS AND ANSWERS

Question: Compare the **themes** in *The Inheritors* and *Free Fall*.

Answer: Both novels deal, in an oblique way, with the condition of modern man. *The Inheritors* conveys the truth that human progress must be moral as well as technical if man is not to be destroyed. *Free Fall*, in its representative modern **protagonist**, illustrates the same need for spiritual and moral awareness. Both novels attack pride and call for self-awareness. The view of history in both novels is a negative one since there are parallel instances of the disintegration of society. The major difference between the two novels is that *The Inheritors*, depicting the blunt consciousness of primitive man, deals with an inevitable stage in the evolution of man which he not only fails to affect but which he cannot even comprehend, while *Free Fall* relies upon the sensitive mind of a modern artist to analyze the very complex problem of individual guilt.

In the sense that **theme** is the expression of why crucial events take place in a novel, the **theme** of *The Inheritors* is a paradox remaining unanswered: the brutality of man inevitably destroys the innocence and beauty of the world, yet man bears responsibility for his actions. *Free Fall* attempts to explain the paradox by saying that man bears responsibility for his actions because he consents to participate in a gradual withdrawal of love from his fellows.

Question: Is *Free Fall* a fable in the way that *The Inheritors* is?

Answer: Traditionally, the fable uses relatively simple characters to illustrate basic moral truths. *The Inheritors* uses such simplification. *Free Fall*, although it is much closer to the **realism** of modern psychological fiction, uses characters in a similarly representative way. Just as Lok and Mal represent youthful inexperience and responsible leadership in *The Inheritors*, so in *Free Fall* Sammy and Nick Shales represent the same contrast, while the other characters are selected as illustrating clearly definable ways of life.

Also, the pattern of discovery is similar in each work. The mind of Lok gradually progresses to the point where, in contemplating the evil works of the Homo sapiens, he begins to make **similes** which suggest an achievement of spiritual insight. Sammy advances to his dark night of the soul in the German prison camp where he suddenly achieves a quality of spiritual awareness. Both characters have discovered the meaning of a world outside and beyond their limited previous existence, and the effect is humanizing.

Question: What is Golding's view of modern society?

Answer: Golding sees in the present world an overdevelopment of technology, competitiveness, violence, and destructiveness and a resulting underdevelopment of ethics. His human characters tend to exist in vacuums which are a result of their selfish preoccupations. In *Free Fall* the general's house which Sammy and Johnny investigate in the darkness in a boyhood adventure later becomes an insane asylum. The suggestion is that life in the military, technologically advanced world leads toward life in an insane asylum. Today we have armies, tomorrow madhouses.

Question: Comment on Golding's ethical view.

Answer: Golding distinguishes between the innocent man and the good man. Lok in *The Inheritors* and young Sammy Mountjoy in *Free Fall* are innocent, but they are incapable of operating in the world in such a way that they would improve society. After Sammy's experience in the prison camp, he becomes the good man, capable of perceiving his relationship to his fellowmen, interested in expiating his guilt, and committed to love.

Question: What, for Golding, is the future of man?

Answer: To some extent Golding is a pessimist. The moral order crumbles while science and technology thrive. Man becomes more and more a cog in a machine which he fails to comprehend. However, such an attitude should be seen as related to his intention of attacking optimistic Darwinian theories of progress. At the same time that he is pointing out the failure of technology, Golding is optimistically constructing a vision of nature and the cosmos which suggests a higher order. The story of Lok is, in itself, a success story, illustrating the progress of the individual in developing new dimensions of consciousness and extended responsibilities for his fellows. And the character of Sammy Mountjoy represents a further advance of self-knowledge and human understanding. So while the world might be afflicted with sin and betrayal, the individual is yet capable of personal progress.

Question: Explain the significance of the titles, *The Inheritors* and *Free Fall*.

Answer: The title, *The Inheritors*, suggests the relationship that exists between the two tribes. The new people inherit the earth from the Neanderthals to make of it what they will. They also inherit some of the primitive qualities as well as some of the spiritual proclivities of the earlier tribe and the responsibilities which they entail. Too, the novel is about modern man, who inherits the conflict depicted as occurring in a prehistorical period and who, although he seems to be going forward, often becomes lost in the same chaos that threatens Tuami's group. Golding seems to be saying that increased technology is useless without an improvement in moral awareness. Further, the title provides an ironic commentary on the earthly condition. Christ promised, in "The Sermon on the Mount," that the meek should inherit the earth. Here, however, the meek Neanderthals are destroyed by the unmeek Homo sapiens. The meek might inherit the heavenly kingdom, but the technologically advanced demand inheritance of the earth.

The ambiguity of the title, *Free Fall*, highlights the central question in the novel. Is the fall of Sammy Mountjoy into sin a freely elected fall or is it the free fall of an object in space? Since Sammy is a representative man, the answer to this question applies to the condition of all men. And that answer, for Golding, is that Sammy is guilty of sin but not of any specific sin. He is responsible for letting his life become a slow drift downward in which the aspirations of his spirit that might find fulfillment in his art are sacrificed to selfish indulgence. He is responsible for the attitude which lets him lose contact with his fellow man and the subsequent network of betrayal.

Question: Discuss symmetry as a structural norm in Golding's fiction.

Answer: In *The Inheritors*, the Neanderthals and the Homo sapiens are balanced against each other. The tribes have similar structures. Their ceremonies are paralleled. Each tribe sees the other as being supernatural in its powers. In *Free Fall*, Sammy in the different periods of his life encounters pairs of antithetical characters who represent important influences: Johnny Spragg and Philip Arnold, Beatrice and Taffy, Rowena Pringle and Nick Shales, Father Watts-Watt and Dr. Halde. This symmetrical effect is appropriate to Golding's dualistic view of the human condition in which man is constantly encountering a choice of darkness or light, spirit or flesh, moral insight or technological advance. Golding, like the mature Sammy Mountjoy, sees it as his purpose to provide a bridge between contrasting and unrelated realms of existence.

Question: Discuss Golding's characterization.

Answer: Most of Golding's characters are flat. That is, they are simple and uncomplicated personalities that do not approach the complexity and roundness of actual life. This is consistent with his purposes as a fabulist who uses his characters to represent easily definable ways of life. However, in his two latest novels, *Free Fall* and *The Spire*, the characters of Sammy Mountjoy and Jocelyn are more complex than previous main figures. This is perhaps to allow Golding to probe, with greater sensitivity, the questions of guilt and responsibility raised in the earlier novels.

But whether they be flat or round, Golding's main characters inevitably develop. Personalities do not remain static but they change and grow and achieve new dimensions. Lok and Sammy Mountjoy both become larger in their humanity and in their powers of spiritual perception. Their personalities are considerably changed at the end of the novel. In a world in flux, the individual has no choice but must change, either in a destructive or in a creative way.

Question: Discuss the symbolism in *The Inheritors* and *Free Fall*.

Answer: In *The Inheritors*, as in *Lord of the Flies*, the natural setting is a source of symbolism. The cave is used to represent the origins of man, the island on which the new people camp is a representation of alienation, the river represents time. In *Free Fall* the emphasis is less on the meaning of symbols than on the meaning of Sammy's existence. But one important symbol is the German prison cell, which represents the confinement of Sammy's spirit by his flesh but which leads him to a discovery, in the dark abyss, of the spiritual life.

Question: To what extent is man free, according to Golding?

Answer: Freedom is always qualified by forces inside and outside of man. Society imposes restrictions and, what is more important, the individual himself is a repository of forces which qualify his freedom. The dark side of man creates a current of fear or lust or greed and these impinge on his ability to direct his life. Only as the individual recognizes the threat to his liberty and accepts, as Sammy does at the end of the novel, the responsibility for directing his life, can he begin to define his rights as a free being and begin to control his destiny. Freedom, then, depends on self-knowledge.

Question: Is Golding a realistic writer?

Answer: In a sense, *Free Fall* is Golding's only realistic novel, that is, it is the only novel in which the experiences described could actually take place without the suspension of laws of nature and probability. But, even in *Free Fall*, Golding is less interested in the reality of actual life than in spiritual and moral reality. It is for this reason that he orders his fiction in the structure of the fable.

Question: Describe the tone of *The Inheritors* and *Free Fall*.

Answer: The tone of *The Inheritors* varies from low-keyed reportage to intense wonder. *Free Fall* focuses on moments of crisis which are analyzed with intensity. Many of the chapters end, not with the strangeness and mystery of *The Inheritors*, but with a highly pitched questioning - "Here, then?" -concerning moral and psychological realities. Both books communicate a sense of the attitude of the author: a scholarly, detached, but compassionate regard for the people he creates.

Question: Is Golding a traditionalist?

Answer: To the extent that he uses a traditional philosophy and ethics and a style reminiscent of the eighteenth-century moral fable, he is. But his main concern is with the modern versions of traditional vices. He sees modern technology, for example, as representing the same temptation to pride that misled the heroes of Greek drama. He sees the failure of human love as universal in time as well as space. In the truths which he discovers, however, there is an ambiguity and complexity which suggest less the traditions of previous philosophies than the attitude of contemporary existentialism.

Stylistically, Golding's writing is actually a mixture of the traditional and the experimental. The form of the fable demands a simplification that is reminiscent of the articulate rationalism of the eighteenth century. Yet, Golding articulates a vision that is complex. In *The Inheritors* he adapts his language to the incomplete minds of the Neanderthals, creating a fragmentary and crude form that demands a participation by the reader in the reconstruction of the reality of existence in an ancient world. In *Free Fall* he renders the consciousness of a man whose clarity of thought is vitiated by his failure of confidence in a rationalistic view of life. Again, the reader must infer from the fragmentary record of Sammy's experiences a harmonious vision of the world.

Question: Comment on the styles of the following passages, the first from *The Inheritors*, the second from *Free Fall*:

He remembered the ice woman. He kept his eyes on the ground lest he should see the awful light and began to crawl away. His body was a dead thing and he could not make it work. He stumbled after Fa and then they were through the crack in the wall and the gully led down in front of them and another crack was the new arrangement of the gap. He fled past Fa and began to fight his way downward.

Then where? I am wise in some ways, can see unusually far through a brick wall and therefore I ought to be able to answer my own question. At least I can tell when I acquired or was given the capacity to see. Dr. Halde attended to that. In freedom I should never have acquired any capacity. Then was loss of freedom the price exacted, a necessary preliminary to a new mode of knowing? But the result of my helplessness out of which came the new mode was also the desperate misery of Beatrice and the good joys of Taffy.

Answer: The first passage records Lok's experiences after the disappearance of Ha. The second records the present searching of Sammy Mountjoy into the meaning of experience just before he recounts his experience with Dr. Halde. The intention in the first passage is to communicate the physical actions of Lok and to suggest his state of fear. The simple structure of sentences, the repeated pronoun "He" followed by a brief predicate, suggest the brute mind of Lok. The brokenness of the thoughts create the context of a mind incomplete, incapable of putting together the data of experience in a meaningful way. The primitive vocabulary heightens the sense of the limited consciousness of Lok.

The second quotation also suggests an incompleteness of mind. Although the language is sophisticated and the questions are intelligent, the mind is hurrying on from question to question without pausing for answer. The words evoke the significant issues in the novel - the question of free will, the problem of self-discovery, the problem of guilt in Sammy's relation to his two women - but without suggesting a solution. The purpose of the passage is not so much to communicate as to perplex.

Question: What part does religion play in the novels *The Inheritors* and *Free Fall*?

Answer: Religion in *The Inheritors* is an essential part of the lives of the Neanderthals. Contrasted with the destructive rituals of the Homo sapiens, the healthy religious activities of Mal and his tribe give form to hunting, eating, burial - to every phase of their lives. And in the framework of their faith, the individual's life is a part of a larger life from which he enters into the world at birth and to which he returns at death. Religion in *Free Fall* is, in its formal aspects, as uncreative as the mutilation ceremonies of the Homo sapiens. Fr. Watts-Watt, the homosexual priest, is a representation of the perverse forms which institutionalized religion can take. On the other hand, the religious instinct is sacred to Golding. Sammy's discovery in prison of the dark places in himself, which are associated with the dimensions of spirit, is the most significant experience in the novel.

Question: Discuss the strategy of point of view in *The Inheritors* and *Free Fall*.

Answer: In *The Inheritors* Golding begins by objectively describing the Neanderthals, allowing himself to move into the minds of the characters. But then, in the middle chapters, he limits his focus to the outlook of Lok, whose adventures are central to the action. Throughout these chapters there is a great deal of dramatic **irony** since the limited mind of Lok cannot deal with the experiences of encountering the new people. The reader must infer for himself that the details which Lok can merely record have a related significance, for example, that the stick which whizzes by Lok is an arrow, that the creature on the island, with the forehead and chin, is a human being, and that the deaths and abductions of the Neanderthals are part of the destructive plan of the Homo sapiens. In the next to the last chapter, the author resorts to a new technique, objectively reporting the last movements of Lok, who is referred to as "it," and who is described concretely as a primitive creature. This is to prepare for the last chapter and the triumph of the Homo sapiens. The world having been inherited by them, the author's outlook shifts to the mind of Tuami, the most "modern" of the creatures of the novel. His thoughts run to the difficult question of the problem of evil in the world and the value of individual action. Thus, Golding adjusts his omniscient author point of view throughout the novel in order to stimulate the reader to a variety of conflicting sympathies and insights concerning the implications of evolutionary change.

In *Free Fall* Golding uses the more concentrated point of view of "I" as **protagonist**. Here the point of view is extremely limited since we are given the reminiscences of the main character as they strike him at a certain time when he is attempting to re-order his past existence. In other words, we are not presented with past actions, but with the present memory of past action treated as it seems to bear upon the compelling issue of the main character's quest for the measure of his guilt. One of the effects of this point of view is to make the story more convincing because of the immediacy of presentation. Another is to involve us intimately in the workings of the mind of the **protagonist** so that we feel we have a nearly perfect knowledge of his psychological identity. Here, the reality of Sammy's mind is at first fragmented and confused, but gradually works toward a harmony of suspended commitment as, after his prisoner of war experiences, he begins to discover the harmony of the universe.

CRITICAL COMMENTARY

EARLY ARTICLES

The numerous articles appearing on Golding in reviews, journals, and quarterlies generally fall into two categories. Several short notes and articles have been written explaining Golding's sources and allusions, for example, his use of R.M. Ballantyne's Coral Island in both *Lord of the Flies* and *Pincher Martin*. The more substantial articles analyze Golding as a fabulist, that is, a writer who arranges characters and events in a symbolic pattern to enforce a moral truth for the benefit of mankind. Occasionally, critics will express reservations with regard to the contrived quality of his symbolism, especially in *Lord of the Flies*, and concerning his traditionalism of **theme**, but the general tendency has been to treat him as a writer of stature. Many distinguished novelists and critics have recognized Golding as an important innovator in the novel form, and there is a steady increase in the number of serious critical studies by those who see in his writing an illumination of human experience of a special sort. His novels are not only a successful **exposition** of the position of modern man threatened by forces of technology and violence that he does not understand, but they also shed light on the perennial plight of man confined in the prison of himself, wrestling with the powers of darkness within.

GOLDING AS SOCIAL CRITIC

Critical commentary on Golding is in the pioneering stage, but its direction seems to be fixed. Since discoveries are being made concerning his handling of sources, it seems probable that with a more extensive analysis of his use of these source materials will come a better appreciation of his attitude to his subject. Often he uses elements from other literature in order to point out some failure in modern society. For example, the **allusions** to Coral Island in *Lord of the Flies* suggest a contrast between the romantic world of that book and the harsh reality of the life of the boys on the island, thus pointing up the absurdity of the romanticism of the boys and of readers of popular escape literature in general. His use of Greek myth, Dante, and Milton often serves to denigrate the modern characters in his novels who fail to fill the heroic mold. Much of the **satire** and social criticism of Golding comes into focus when we understand his use of these other books and traditions as ironic commentary in his own novel.

The more that his novels are compared, the more apparent becomes the application of his ideas to modern society. In every book there is the expression of the danger of technology, whether in the hands of primitive hunters or the sophisticated Dr. Halde, as a cruel and destructive force. There is a corresponding insistence on the need for self-awareness and for moral advancement.

THE FORM OF THE NOVELS

Another avenue of investigation that is opening concerns the form that Golding creates. He overturns many of the **conventions** of the novel in order to allow himself unprecedented freedom.

He brings the supernatural to the novels as a directing force. He uses fate for the same purpose. Instead of arranging events in a chain of causes and effects, he structures his novels in a ritual pattern, using processions, pilgrimages, and the offering of sacrifices as dramatic climaxes. He includes explicit commentary on philosophical and moral issues, such as the question of free will. He uses hallucination as a device for exploring worlds other than the real one. He extends dramatic **irony** to the breaking point. He mixes elements from religious tradition with those from the fields of psychology and anthropology. The primitive urges of man and the rituals which give them form are associated with religious symbolism so that, for example, the snake which represents the id also stands for original sin, and the pig-killing ceremony of the boys, with its circular formation and rhythmic chant, resembles a formal religious service. The offering of a sacrifice of a part of the kill reinforces the relation of the hunt to religious practices. In general, his adaptation of elements from the Greek drama is the most distinctive large-scale innovation made by Golding in the novel form.

FATE

In the novels, spiritual forces play an important part in the lives of men. Because Golding believes in a spiritual destiny, he lets the action be controlled by a divine puppeteer. Events like the landing of the dead parachutist on the island in *Lord of the Flies*, and the arrival of the naval officer in time to save Ralph's life are as deliberately implausible as the entrance of a god from a machine at the end of a Greek play. Their purpose is to illustrate the presence of the forces of fate, which act counter to the individual's desire to control his own life. The storm in *Pincher Martin*, and the unique circumstances of Sammy in the prison camp in *Free Fall*, willing to confess but lacking information, are further instances of the manipulation of the individual by forces operating in violation of the laws of probability.

SELF-DISCOVERY

Because the most important **theme** in his novels is the need for man to know himself, Golding develops his novels towards moments of intense psychological experience, in which an isolated character sees in his surroundings a representation of the destructive powers present in himself. Both Simon and Ralph in *Lord of the Flies* come to such realizations as they look at the skull of the sow. In *The Inheritors*, moments of illumination come to Lok after his flight from the new people and to Tuami at the end of the novel. It is ironic that Lok should find his "self" in encountering the new people, and that Tuami should derive, from his battle with the Neanderthals, a sense of his own barbarity. In *Pincher Martin* the **climax** is Christopher's realization, as the black lightning singles him out for death, of his own nothingness. In *Free Fall* the moment of crisis is Sammy's experience as a prisoner of war when, confined in a dark cell, he discovers a slimy, flesh-like object on the floor, which causes him to come to a realization of the foul deformity that exists within himself. Golding tries to give these moments of self-discovery the force that the revelation scenes have in Greek tragedy.

THE FALL OF THE PROUD

Often in Greek drama the hero suffers from hubris, a blind pride that leads him to ignore the moral law until eventually he meets with a tragic downfall. In three of Golding's novels, *Lord of the Flies*, *Pincher Martin*, and *Free Fall*, the chief characters suffer from a blind pride which seems to put them above the traditional restraints of human society. In his other novel, *The Inheritors*, it is the secondary group of characters, Homo sapiens, who suffer from hubris. Not until the end of each novel do these characters see themselves as they are, and then it is too late to rectify the damage they have done. And they are often too late to save themselves.

The violent punishments that some of Golding's characters undergo might seem too strong for their crimes. The implication is that the world is not a place of justice. This becomes especially apparent when we consider the fates of such innocent characters as Simon in *Lord of the Flies* and Beatrice in *Free Fall*, or the entire tribe of Neanderthal men, who seem to be so attractive and peace loving, in *The Inheritors*. Although all of these characters are lacking in self-knowledge, they commit no crimes to merit their violent extermination as complete human beings. What Golding is saying is that the world can be a very cruel place where the least protected are the easiest victims. But he does see the possibility of a better world. In "A Conversation with Golding" he is reported as saying that he "would have liked Ralph to 'make it,' but he couldn't. The 'nice guy' frequently loses." In the island society the boys lack the forms of justice that might protect them from destruction. There are, however, other societies where justice can prevail, although only under special circumstances. "After all it's only when you have a fairly protected society-as America has been for most of its existence-that you can develop a genuinely fair society." Golding's novels attempt to strengthen the forms of human behavior, both individual and social, that provide the climate for justice and freedom.

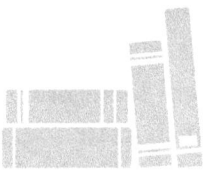

BIBLIOGRAPHY

Baker, James R., and Arthur P. Ziegler, eds., Casebook Edition of William Golding's "Lord of the Flies": *Text, Criticism, and Notes*, New York: Putnam's 1964.

_____, *William Golding, A Critical Study*, New York: St. Martin's, 1965. Analyzes the ideas and form of the four novels and the play. Sees Golding as a rationalist and a formal realist who depends strongly on classical literary materials. Contains a nearly complete bibliography of Golding's work and an annotated bibliography of secondary studies.

Broes, Arthur T., "The Two Worlds of William Golding," *Lectures on Modern Novelists*. Carnegie Series in English, No. 7, Pittsburgh, Pa.: Dept. of English, Carnegie Institute of Technology, 1963.

Bufkin, Ernest Claude, Jr., "The Novels of William Colding: A Descriptive and Analytic Study," *Dissertation Abstracts*, XXV, 469-470. A Vanderbilt University dissertation. 1964.

Cox, C. B., "*Lord of the Flies*," *Critical Quarterly*, II (1960), 112-117.

Davis, Douglas, "A Conversation with Golding." *The New Republic*, (May 4, 1963), 28-30.

Drew, Philip, "Second Reading," *Cambridge Review*, LXXVIII (1956), 79-84.

Forster, E. M., "Introduction," *Lord of the Flies*, New York: Coward-McCann, 1962, pp. ix-xii. A brief introduction to Golding's method.

Freedman, Ralph, "The New **Realism**: The Fancy of William Golding," *Perspective*, X (1958), 118-128.

Gindin, James, "'Gimmick' and **Metaphor** in the Novels of William Golding," *Modern Fiction Studies*, VI (1960), 145-152.

Golding, William, and Frank Kermode, "The Meaning of it All," *Books and Bookmen*, V (October, 1959), pp. 9-10. A BBC radio interview in which Golding discusses his first three novels.

Green, Martin, "Distaste for the Contemporary," *Nation*, CXC (May 21, 1960), 451-454.

Green, Peter, "The World of William Golding," *Review of English Literature*, I, ii (1960), 62-72.

Gregor, Ian, and Mark Kinkead-Weekes, "The Strange Case of Mr. Golding and His Critics," *Twentieth Century*, CLXVII (1960), 115-125. Analyzes *Free Fall*.

Hynes, Sam, "Novels of a Religious Man," *Commonwealth*, LXXI (March 18, 1960), 673-675.

———, *William Golding*, New York: Columbia University Press, 1964. Describes Golding's novels as transcending the **genre** of moral fable because of their unique intensity and complexity. Analyzes the symbolism and style of the novels.

Karl, Frederick R., "The Novel as Moral Allegory: The Fiction of William Golding, Iris Murdoch, Rex Warner, and P. H. Newby," *The Contemporary English Novel*, New York: The Noonday Press, 1962.

Kermode, Frank, "The Novels of William Golding," *International Literary Annual*, III (1961), 11-29.

Kermode, Frank, "The Novels of William Golding," *International Literary Annual*, III (1961), 11-29. On the first four novels.

MacLure, Millar, "Allegories of Innocence," *Dalhousie Review*, XL (1960), 145-156.

MacShane, Frank, "The Novels of William Golding," *Dalhousie Review*, XLII (1962), 171-183.

Marcus, Steven, "The Novel Again," *Partisan Review*, XXIX (Spring, 1962), pp. 171-195. Stresses the poetic in Golding and other modern novelists.

Nelson, William, ed., *William Golding's "Lord of the Flies": A Source Book*, New York: The Odyssey Press, 1963. Reviews, articles, and excerpts from sources.

Niemeyer, Carl, "The Coral Island Revisited," *College English*, XXII (1961), 241-245.

Peter, John, "The Fables of William Golding," *Kenyon Review*, XIX (1957), 577-592.

Quinn, Michael, "An Unheroic Hero: William Golding's Pincher Martin," *Critical Quarterly*, IV (1962), 247-256.

Rosenfield, Claire, "'Men of a Smaller Growth': A Psychological Analysis of William Golding's *Lord of the Flies*," *Literature and Psychology*, XI (1961), 93-101.

Sullivan, Walter, "William Golding: The Fables and the Art," *Sewanee Review*, LXXI (1963), 660-664.

Wain, John, "Lord of the Agonies," *Aspect*, I (1963), 56-57.

Walters, Margaret, "Two Fabulists: Golding and Camus," *Melbourne Critical Review*, No. 4 (1961), 18-29.

EXPLORE THE ENTIRE LIBRARY OF BRIGHT NOTES STUDY GUIDES

From Shakespeare to Sinclair Lewis and from Plato to Pearl S. Buck, The Bright Notes Study Guide library spans hundreds of volumes, providing clear and comprehensive insights into the world's greatest literature. Discover more, faster with the Bright Notes Study Guide to the classics you're reading today.

See the entire library of available
Bright Notes guides at **BrightNotes.com**

Available in print and digital wherever books are sold

IP INFLUENCE PUBLISHERS

www.ingramcontent.com/pod-product-compliance
Lightning Source LLC
LaVergne TN
LVHW011708060526
838200LV00051B/2801